```
BIG BEND ON THE RIO GRANDE    B
IOGRAPHY OF A NATIONAL PARK


JAMESON, JOHN R.   1945-


F392.B53J36 1987
                              SC
```

Big Bend on the Rio Grande

American University Studies

Series IX
History

Vol. 18

PETER LANG
New York · Bern · Frankfurt am Main · Paris

John R. Jameson

Big Bend on the Rio Grande

Biography of a National Park

PETER LANG
New York · Bern · Frankfurt am Main · Paris

Library of Congress Cataloging-in-Publication Data

Jameson, John R.
   Big Bend on the Rio Grande.

   (American university studies. Series IX, History; vol. 18)
   Bibliography: p.
   Includes index.
   1. Big Bend National park (Tex.)—History.
   I. Title. II. Series.
   F392.B53J36   1987   976.4'932   86-27686
   ISBN 0-8204-0300-8
   ISSN 0740-0462

CIP-Kurztitelaufnahme der Deutschen Bibliothek

Jameson, John R.:
Big Bend on the Rio Grande: biography of a national park / John R. Jameson. – New York; Bern; Frankfurt am Main; Paris: Lang, 1987.
   (American University Studies: Ser. 9, History; Vol. 18)
   ISBN 0-8204-0300-8

NE: American University Studies / 09

© Peter Lang Publishing, Inc., New York 1987

All rights reserved.
Reprint or reproduction, even partially, in all forms such as microfilm, xerography, microfiche, microcard, offset strictly prohibited.

Printed by Weihert-Druck GmbH, Darmstadt, West Germany

For my parents, who first introduced me to Big Bend National Park, and in memory of Clifford B. Casey (1897–1986), the Big Bend Country's foremost historian.

Table of Contents

Preface	ix
Chapter I. The Quest	1
Chapter II. The Politics of Fund Raising	19
Chapter III. Land Acquisition	39
Chapter IV. The Publicity Campaign	49
Chapter V. The Ideal and the Reality	69
Chapter VI. Ranchers and Predators	85
Chapter VII. Life on the Last Frontier	97
Chapter VIII. National or International Park?	113
Epilogue	127
Appendix	
Map of Big Bend National Park	133
Public No. 157–74th Congress [S. 2131]	134
Big Bend National Park Chronology	135
Big Bend Annual Visitation Figures, 1944–1985	138
Visits to U. S. National Parks 1976–1977	140
Responses to Wilderness Recommendations	142
Decimal Classifications, Record Group 79	143
Bibliography	153
Index	165

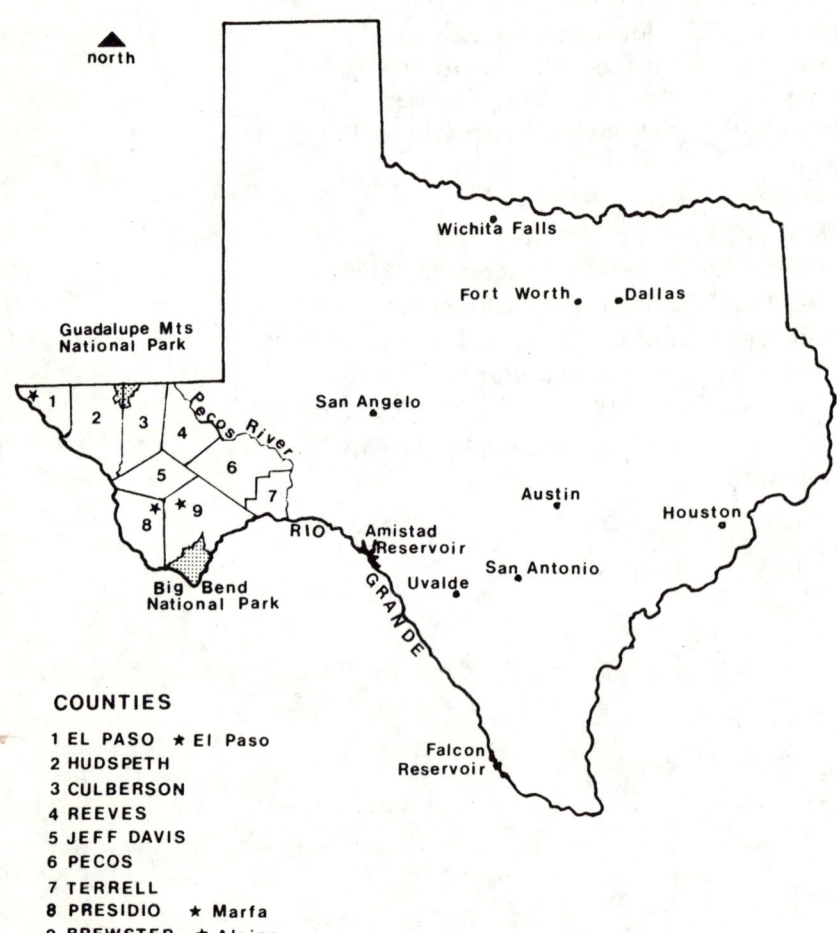

Preface

In 1968 historian Roderick Nash called attention to the need for more individual histories of America's national parks. Many books, pamphlets, and articles have been written about the Big Bend country's geology, flora and fauna, folklore and legends, archaeology, and history, but none of these examine more than one aspect or two of the park's history. For example, one of the best books on the region is Ronnie C. Tyler's *The Big Bend: A History of the Last Texas Frontier* (1975), which has only one chapter that specifically deals with the park. This study, then, is a response to Nash's plea. It is not a history of the region, but rather focuses on the park itself; hence the title, "Big Bend on the Rio Grande: Biography of a National Park." As such, it emphasizes the five decades from the 1930s into the 1980s with particular concern for people's perceptions of and attitudes toward national parks in general while examining one in particular. Other subjects considered include the publicity and fund raising campaigns, land acquisition, visitor and employee experiences on the "last frontier," development plans for the park, and the idea for an international park on the Rio Grande. In addition, it provides a revealing case study of an important federal agency, the National Park Service.

The generous assistance, encouragement, and inspiration of several individuals and institutions have helped make this work possible. Back in the summer of 1955 my parents kindled my love for the Big Bend Country when they packed all six of us into our two-door Ford and drove through the desert heat for what seemed like an eternity before we reached the coolness of the Chisos Basin in the park. From that moment on I have been under the Big Bend's spell. W. Eugene Hollon, Professor Emeritus, University of Toledo, first apprised me of the richness of the Big Bend resources in the National Archives. He made a special trip to the capital and while there perused the files, where he found several important documents on historian Walter Prescott Webb's involvement in the park's publicity campaign (see pages 55–59). Patrick Barkey, Director Emeritus of the University of Toledo Library, greatly facilitated my research when his institution funded the microfilming of a major archival collection. Especially helpful were the people of the National Park Service. The Washington, Santa Fe, and Big Bend staffs unhesitatingly replied to even the most vague queries. Bill M. Collins and Jess Caldwell of the Texas Parks and Wildlife Department went well beyond the call of duty. Mr. Collins ran down documents in his agency's Austin office that proved invaluable, particularly in chapters one, two, and three. Mr. Caldwell personally assisted me in the Bastrop State Park Warehouse risking life and limb to retrieve rather heavy file boxes from ceiling shelves. Ross Maxwell, the first superintendent at Big Bend, graciously invited me into his Austin home for an interview and corresponded with me about the park's early years. A good friend of his, Robert Wear, who covered the park movement for the Fort Worth *Star-Telegram* after World War II, likewise freely shared with yours truly his experiences in the Big Bend country. Ronnie C. Tyler, former Curator of History, Amon Carter Museum and now Director, Texas State Historical Association, not only opened his files but also gave new perspectives on the use of visual historical documents. Two individuals have given permission to reproduce their photographs in the book, Cindy L. Marquez of Sul Ross State University and Mary Moody of Denison, Texas. Mrs. Moody's artistic skill with a camera revealed another dimension of Big Bend's hauntingly beautiful landscape. Robert Kvasnicka of the National Archives Building in Washington, D.C. saved days of work with his knowledge of natural resource records. Without his assistance, I would have overlooked several important collections. Two very special people are Ernest and Marie Dickinson of Pottsboro, Texas (my wife's parents) who not only are fine cartographers, but also let me stay at their lake house for an enjoyable and productive spring during which I began work on the Big Bend manuscript.

    Administrators, faculty, staff, and students at Washington State University have also been most supportive. Two of my colleagues in the Department of History, David H. Stratton, past Chair, and Richard L. Hume, Chair, have cajoled and encouraged me at each step to see the project through to completion. In Spring 1980, the University awarded me a faculty travel grant, which allowed me to return one more time to Washington, D.C. In addition, the Provost's Office, the History Development Fund, and the Dean's Office, Humanities and Social Sciences Division, College of Sciences and Arts provided the financial resources so necessary to carry on scholarly research and publishing. At the Humanities Research Center, Thomas C. Faulkner, Director, Rhonda Blair, Administrative Assistant, and Hongbo Tan, Research Assistant, offered their state of the art facilities and computer equipment to prepare the manuscript for publication. June Hanley, my word processor, likewise performed yeoman service from the first through the final drafts.

I am also grateful to the editors of *The Public Historian*, the West Texas Historical Association *Year Book*, the Texas Western Press, and the University of Toledo Press for permission to use ideas or portions of the manuscript first published in their journals, series, or anthology. The full citations are given in the bibliography.

And last, but not least, I want to thank my wife, Suzy and sons, John, Jr., and Andrew, who also have a fond place in their hearts for Big Bend (even from the distant reaches of the State of Washington). Of course, any errors of fact or interpretation are my own responsibility.

JRJ
Pullman, WA

I The Quest

In 1935 some six decades after the establishment of Yellowstone National Park, Texas finally obtained its first national park. The long wait hardly seems worthy of additional comment since many states even today still lack a national park while the Lone Star State has two—Big Bend and Guadalupe Mountains. But what justifies a further examination is that Texans had unsuccessfully tried since the first of this century to secure a national park. And the area eventually designated for a park was the most unexpected and least known of the various proposals considered.

United States Congressman John H. Stephens from Wichita Falls was one of the first to seek a national park for Texas. In January 1908 he introduced in the House of Representatives a bill for the creation of Palo Duro Canyon National Forest Reserve and Park. The Congressman considered the area "the finest natural park in the entire Southwest." Seven years later Stephens complained before the House that Texas, then the largest state in the union, still had neither a national park nor a forest reserve.[1]

Stephen's plan received support throughout the Texas Panhandle and Red River regions of Texas, Oklahoma, and Louisiana. The local press, chambers of commerce, and the Texas Federation of Women's Clubs endorsed the Palo Duro project. However, the most politically influential group was the Red River Improvement

---

1. He could have also added that Texas lacked a national monument. U. S. Congress, House, H. R. 11749, 60th Cong., 1st sess., 1908, p. 480; U. S. Congress, House, H. R. 13651, 60th Cong., 2nd sess., 1908, p. 706; U. S. Congress, House, 64th Cong., 2nd sess., 1917, Appendix and Index, p. 305. Stephens also introduced similar bills in 1911 and 1915. See U. S. Congress, House, H. R. 4734, 62nd Cong., 1st sess., 1911, p. 245; U. S. Congress, House, H. R. 330, 64th Cong., 1st sess., 1915, p. 21.

Association whose membership included congressmen whose districts bordered on the Red River. The president of this organization was Morris Sheppard, later to become a United States Senator, and one of the most staunch advocates for a national park in Texas.[2]

Yet even with such substantial backing, Stephen's proposal had little chance for success. He wanted to combine the utilitarian function of a national forest watershed with that of a national park for aesthetic and recreational purposes. His plan required the cooperation of rival federal bureaus, the Forest Service in the Department of Agriculture and the newly created National Park Service (1916) in the Department of the Interior. In the sensitive years following the Hetch Hetchy controversy where the Forest Service's Gifford Pinchot had defended the construction of a water reservoir in Yosemite National Park for the city of San Francisco, such cooperation between ideologically opposed agencies was too much to hope for. If Stephens had presented separate bills, one for a national park at the canyon and the other for a national forest along the Red River, perhaps he would have had more success. Unfortunately, such an alternative never presented itself before his retirement from politics in 1918.[3]

There was much activity directed toward the creation of national and state parks at the state level during and after the 1920s. In 1923 Governor Pat Neff urged the legislature to form a state parks board to begin the acquisition of a system of state parks. But other than the creation of such a board, Neff's suggestion got nowhere. The thirty-third legislature appropriated no funds for park purchase or maintenance. Seven years later during the early stages of the great depression, the State Democratic Convention in Galveston endorsed the idea of state parks in Texas. In addition, the convention called upon Texas's representatives in Congress to ask the federal government to establish at least one national park in the state. Governor Ross Sterling also echoed the call for parks in his inaugural address in 1931.[4]

---

2. U. S. Congress, House, 64th Cong., 2nd sess., 1917, Appendix and Index, p. 305.

3. *Ibid.*; Roderick Nash, *Wilderness and the American Mind* (rev. ed.; New Haven: Yale University Press, 1973), chapter ten.

4. Victor H. Schoffelmayer, "The Big Bend Area of Texas," *Texas Geographic Magazine*, 1 (May., 1937), p. 5. The Executive Secretary of the Texas State Parks Board wrote an excellent article on state park developments in Texas

The newly authorized Emergency Conservation Work agency (ECW), created by an act of Congress on March 31, 1933, had much to do with the increased activity of the legislature in an area where it had previously shown little concern. During the years preceding World War II, the Texas legislature established over three dozen state parks. The ECW—more popularly known as the Civilian Conservation Corps or CCC—set up camps in most national and certain designated state parks and provided funds for their operation and development. At the same time the CCC created hundreds of jobs for the nation's unemployed.[5]

Meanwhile, in the early 1930s the Texas legislature adopted two resolutions concerning a national park for the state. In 1931, Senate Concurrent Resolution 9 called for "an immediate survey" to determine if Texas's scenic areas measured up to national park standards. Senate Concurrent Resolution 73, adopted two years later, pointed out that the state still did not have a national park or forest and called for their creation "in order to assist the unemployment situation in Texas."[6]

Senator Morris Sheppard further pursued the matter of a national park for Texas and sent a copy of SCR 9 to Secretary of the

---

through the 1930s. See William J. Lawson and Will Mann Richardson, "The Texas State Park System: A History, Study of Development and Plans for the Future of the Texas State Parks," *Texas Geographic Magazine*, 11 (December, 1938), pp. 1-12; *Journal of the Senate of Texas*, S. C. R. 9, 42nd Legislature, reg. sess., pp. 97-98.

5. On March 21, 1933 when President Franklin D. Roosevelt first introduced the bill for the creation of the Emergency Conservation Work agency (ECW), he used the name Civilian Conservation Corps (CCC). However, it did not become statutory until June 28, 1937. See John A. Salmond, *The Civilian Conservation Corps, 1933-1942: A New Deal Case Study* (Durham, N. C.: Duke University Press, 1967), p. 26. Pamphlets issued by the Texas State Parks Board in the 1940s expressed the debt owed to the CCC for Texas's fine system of state parks. See "Guide to State Parks of Texas," November, 1941, File 601, Part I, Records of Big Bend National Park, Record Group 79, National Archives Building (hereafter cited as BBNP, RG 79, NA).

6. *Journal of the Senate of Texas*, S. C. R. 9, 42nd Legislature, reg. sess., pp. 97-98; *Journal of the Senate of Texas*, S. C. R. 73, 43rd Legislature, reg. sess., p. 1935. Senator Morris Sheppard had SCR 9 published in its entirety in the *Congressional Record* and Representative John Nance Garner referred to SCR 9's request for a survey for a national park in a memorial statement. U. S. Congress, Senate, 71st Cong., 3rd sess., 1931, p. 4001; U. S. Congress, House, 71st Cong., 3rd sess., 1931, p. 6213.

Interior Ray Lyman Wilbur. "Please let me know," he asked, "if the survey requested [by SCR 9] can be made at an early date." The Secretary gave Sheppard's letter to Horace M. Albright, Director of the National Park Service. In his reply Albright told the Senator that the Park Service had six park projects pending in Texas—Davis Mountains in Jeff Davis County, Guadalupe in Culberson and Hudspeth Counties, McKittrick Canyon in Culberson County, Palo Duro in Randall County, Alto Frio Canyon in Uvalde County, and Texas within Jeff Davis, Brewster, Presidio, Pecos, Culberson, and Hudspeth Counties. He further indicated that his agency would eventually investigate each of these proposals to determine if they met the exacting standards necessary for a national park. Albright also reminded the Senator that the NPS had "almost one hundred other proposed projects on record for investigation, some with very decided priority rights."[7]

The reply was hardly encouraging, yet Albright's negative attitude went even deeper than the tone of the letter implied. Shortly before the Director had written Sheppard, he had confessed to a private correspondent his strong disapproval of such measures as SCR 9 and cited an adverse Park Service report written in regard to a similar request from the state of Florida: "The underlying idea of the bill is the selection of a National Park within a State, thereby perhaps stressing the idea of location for a park rather than the idea of scenic grandeur irrespective of state lines." Albright then commented that if the scenery in a state was not already nationally recognized, "there was no use to hunt for it" as a national park site. Obviously he feared that the country could become burdened with parks that were national in name only.[8] Albright had good reason for his belief since several inferior areas had been made into national parks.[9]

---

7. Sheppard to Ray Lyman Wilbur, February 24, 1931, File 0-32, Part I, BBNP, RG 79, NA; Albright to Sheppard, March 2, 1931, File 0-32, Part I, BBNP, RG 79, NA.

8. Albright to Vance Prather, February 3, 1931, File 0-32, Part I, BBNP, RG 79, NA.

9. Before there were any real guidelines for the establishment of national parks, Congress authorized three inferior parks: Wind Cave in the Black Hills of South Dakota, Sullys Hill in North Dakota, and Platt in Oklahoma. See John Ise, *Our National Park Policy: A Critical History* (Baltimore: The Johns Hopkins

Santa Elena Canyon on the Rio Grande (©Mary Moody)

The Director's yardstick for the designation of a national park was that the prospective site must have "scenery of quality so unusual and impressive, or natural features so extraordinary as to possess national interest and importance as contradistinguished from merely local interest."[10] These are indeed worthy criteria, but they expressed a certain degree of close-mindedness in regard to America's natural scenic resources. Albright assumed that there existed no remote areas of outstanding natural beauty or national worth that remained virtually unknown to the local citizenry as well as to the Park Service. But at least two such places did exist: the Everglades of Florida and the Big Bend country of Texas. The latter was so isolated that one local resident estimated that ninety-nine per cent of his fellow Texans did not know of the existence of the area and its striking scenic and natural attractions.[11] This was perhaps somewhat of an exaggeration, but if applied to the NPS it represented understatement. For the Park Service was still unaware of the merits of the Big Bend country.

The NPS concentrated instead on other areas in West Texas. The first location in Texas which actually received serious consideration as a national park site was the Guadalupe Mountains. The Park Service viewed them as a possible extension to Carlsbad Caverns National Park or as a separate national park. However, nothing was accomplished about the matter until the creation of Guadalupe Mountains National Park in 1966. Of the five other sites in Texas under investigation by the NPS, none prior to 1934 specifically included the geographical landmarks in Brewster County that today comprise Big Bend National Park. These features are the Chisos Mountains and the three canyons on the Rio Grande—Boquillas, Santa Elena, and Mariscal.[12]

Press, 1961), chapter six.

10. Albright to Prather, February 3, 1931, File 0-32, Part 1, BBNP, RG 79, NA.

11. C. B. Casey and Lewis H. Saxton, "The Life of Everett Ewing Townsend," *West Texas Historical and Scientific Society Publication* No. 17 (1958), p. 54.

12. U. S., Department of Interior, *Annual Report of the Secretary of the Interior, for the fiscal year ended June 30, 1933* (Washington, D. C.: Government Printing Office, 1933), p. 165; U. S., Department of Interior, *Annual Report of the Secretary of the Interior, for the fiscal year ended June 30, 1934* (Washington, D.

Lodge in Chisos Basin; Casa Grande in background   (©Mary Moody)

Of the six proposals the NPS regarded Texas National Park as the one which eventually became Big Bend.[13] The original idea for Texas National Park is attributed to United States Congressman C. B. Hudspeth of El Paso. In 1924 and again in 1929 he introduced a bill for the creation of a national park in Jeff Davis County. Hudspeth's proposals died in the Committee on the Public Lands.[14]

The Texas National Park idea emerged again in 1933 when the owner of 23,000 acres in Presidio County offered to donate land for a state park if the legislature would cancel a $10,000 debt he owed the state. When the legislature refused, D. E. Colp, chairman of the Texas State Parks Board, informed the Park Service of the legislature's inaction. He hoped that the federal government would purchase the land for park purposes. However, Colp doomed the chances of this happening when he told the Park Service's Conrad Wirth that if the TSPB had received the acreage, it would have developed the land for recreational purposes rather than for its scenic worth. "Apparently," Wirth concluded, "this area is not of national park standards." It was removed from the list of proposed parks in January 1933.[15]

Obviously, the 23,000 acres in Presidio County and Hudspeth's proposal for a park in Jeff Davis County did not include the site in southern Brewster County that today is Big Bend National Park. The site of the proposed Texas National Park was located within six of the largest counties in the state. The extensive area (25,460 square miles) contained three of the other proposed parks. The vagueness of the Texas National Park area indicated that the Park Service still had no awareness of the Big Bend Country as of January 1933.[16]

The Big Bend country began to receive attention in February 1933 during the session of the 43rd Texas legislature. Abilene's Rep-

---

C.: Government Printing Office, 1934), p. 176.

13. "Review of Proposed Big Bend National Park," May 1, 1934, File 0-32, Part I, BBNP, RG 79, NA; "Status Report on Texas National Park" (no date), File 0-32, Part VIII, BBNP, RG 79, NA.

14. U. S. Congress, House, H. R. 9193, 68th Cong., 1st sess., 1924, p. 8497; U. S. Congress, House, H. R. 3590, 71st Cong., 1st sess., 1929, p. 2303.

15. "Review of Proposed Texas National Park," January 19, 1933, File 0-32, Part I, BBNP, RG 79, NA.

16. The three proposed parks in the area of Texas National Park were Guadalupe Mountains, McKittrick Canyon, and Davis Mountains.

resentative R. M. Wagstaff had read an edition of *Nature Magazine* which devoted the entire issue to Texas. An article by J. Frank Dobie noted that the Lone Star State had not set aside any of its public lands for park purposes. He included among ideal prospective sites the hill country, the coastal areas, and the "wild Big Bend." Another story in the journal specifically concerned the Big Bend country and throughout the magazine were photographs of the region's magnificent canyons. The pictures and articles so impressed Wagstaff that he questioned E. E. Townsend, the representative from Brewster County, about their accuracy. Townsend replied affirmatively and Wagstaff purportedly said, "Then why don't you do something about it?" Wagstaff now regarded the Big Bend as having the potential of becoming "one of the grandest parks in the nation."[17]

Townsend needed no convincing since he had been saying the same thing for almost fifty years. As far back as the summer of 1894 when he had worked as a river guard he visited the Chisos Mountains for the first time and was so overwhelmed that he observed that he had seen God as never before. He vowed that if he could ever afford it he would buy the whole Chisos Mountains for himself and friends, and when no longer wanted he would give it to the state.[18] As the years passed, Townsend steadfastly held on to his vision. But as it became apparent that he would never be able to purchase the area, he realized there was "little hope of ever seeing it [a park]put through as a State or Governmental development."[19] Suddenly Wagstaff's

---

17. Wagstaff and Townsend relate slightly different versions of this episode. Townsend credited Robert T. Hill's "Running the Cañons of the Rio Grande: A Chapter of Recent Exploration," *Century Magazine*, January 1901, pp. 371–387 with influencing Wagstaff. See Casey and Saxton, "The Life of Everett Ewing Townsend," p. 52. Wagstaff in a newspaper interview in 1944 and later in a journal article recounted that he first read of the Big Bend region in *Nature Magazine*, December 1930 and decided to introduce legislation for a state park during the 1931 legislative session. However, because of the possibility of the reinstatement of forfeited lands in the Big Bend, Wagstaff waited until the next legislative session before introducing the proposal. See Abilene *Reporter-News*, June 11, 1944; R. M. Wagstaff, "Beginnings of the Big Bend Park," West Texas Historical Association *Year Book*, XLIV (October, 1968), pp. 3–14.

18. Virginia Madison, *The Big Bend Country of Texas* (2nd ed.; New York: October House, 1968), p. 230.

19. E. E. Townsend to Col. Robert H. Lewis, November 25, 1933, File 207, BBNP, RG 79, NA.

interest in Townsend's dream revived the project.[20]

Wagstaff and Townsend introduced House Bill 771 before the legislature on March 2, 1933. The bill easily passed and on May 27 Governor "Ma" Ferguson signed it. The new act created Texas Canyons State Park on fifteen sections of land in the proximity of Santa Elena, Mariscal, and Boquillas Canyons. These acres, previously under the auspices of the Permanent School Fund, now became the responsibility of the Texas State Parks Board.[21]

Three months later Congressman Ewing Thomason notified Townsend that President Franklin D. Roosevelt had approved four CCC camps for Texas, one "near Big Bend Park in Brewster County." Later Wagstaff and Townsend individually introduced legislation to increase the size of the park, keeping the term "Big Bend" instead of "Texas Canyons." The combined bill passed both houses and Governor Ferguson signed it on October 27, 1933. Under its provisions, 150,000 acres of unsold public free school land at a value of one cent per acre was transferred to the Texas State Parks Board. At the same time $1,500 from the General Revenue fund was to be paid to the School Fund which retained all mineral rights to the land. In addition, tax delinquent lands in the area became eligible for park purposes. With a potential 225,000 acres, Big Bend now ranked as Texas's largest state park.[22]

Townsend still was not content with anything less than a national park for Texas and during the summer and fall of 1933 he

---

20. Although E. E. Townsend is considered the "father" of the idea and the reality of Big Bend National Park, others also saw the park potential of the region. For instance, Sgt. Jodie P. Harris, stationed with Company I, Fourth Texas Infantry at Stillwell Crossing in 1916 wrote about the possibilities for a national park in his service newspaper, *The Big Bend*. Harris also drew postcards for his relatives which depicted the same theme. See Fort Worth *Star-Telegram*, October 10, 1937; April 6, 1958. There were others (see Harry Connelly, "Big Bend National Park Project Reality at Last," *West Texas Today*, September, 1941), but in light of Townsend's numerous contributions to the park movement, he fully deserves his designation as father of Big Bend National Park.

21. Casey and Saxton, "The Life of Everett Ewing Townsend," p. 54; Casey, "The Big Bend National Park," West Texas Historical and Scientific Society *Publication* No. 13 (1948), p. 30; *Vernon's Texas Statutes 1948*, Art. 6077b.

22. Casey, "The Big Bend National Park," p. 31; "Historical Summary of Big Bend Legislation" (no date), Box A-11, Bastrop State Park Warehouse, Bastrop, Texas (hereafter cited as Bastrop SPW); *Vernon's Texas Statutes 1948*, Art. 6077c.

E.E. Townsend, father of Big Bend National Park
(©C.B. Casey Collection, Archives of the Big Bend, Sul Rass State University)

forwarded a barrage of letters and photographs to the Park Service extolling the virtues of the Big Bend country. Due to Townsend's propaganda effort and also the proposed establishment of a CCC camp in the region, the still relatively unknown area finally came to the attention of the NPS. The Park Service had the responsibility of designating and supervising CCC camps in state and national parks. Roger Toll, chief investigator for the NPS, visited the Big Bend country during four days in January 1934 accompanied by Townsend, J. Evetts Haley, and others. Toll's subsequent report endorsed the Big Bend area for a national park and called it "decidedly the outstanding scenic area of Texas." He further remarked that it "gives promise of becoming one of the noted scenic spectacles of the United States." The National Park official also recommended the construction of CCC camps at Santa Elena Canyon, since the chance of finding water in the Chisos Basin appeared limited.[23]

Toll was born and raised in Denver, Colorado and began his Park Service career in 1919. Over the next decade he served as superintendent of Mount Rainier, Rocky Mountain, and Yellowstone National Parks. He prided himself on having climbed all of the fifty peaks within Rocky Mountain National Park during his tenure there. His appreciation of aesthetic natural beauty was not restricted by his own experiences in the Rocky Mountain West or along the northwest Pacific coast. Indeed, he possessed the uncommon ability to find natural beauty where others, unaccustomed to an unfamiliar environment, might only see the bruising, cutting, and arid nature of the land. Also, Toll's aesthetic sense surmounted what seemed a prerequisite for most of the early parks, a preoccupation with nature's strange and unusual creations. To some observers, the Big Bend represented only harsh mediocrity, for it contained neither the highest peak in Texas nor were its canyons anywhere near as deep as the Grand Canyon in Arizona. Yet Toll immediately comprehended the unusual, compelling beauty that the local residents had long

---

23. Alpine *Avalanche*, September 3, 1948. Townsend used many of W. D. Smithers's photographs, the dean of the Big Bend photographers. Representative samples of his work can be found in his book, *Chronicles of the Big Bend: A Photographic Memoir of Life on the Border* (Austin: Madrona Press, Inc., 1976). "Report on the Proposed Big Bend National Park," March 3, 1934, File 207, BBNP, RG 79, NA; Toll to Herbert Maier, February 19, 1934, File 0-32, Part I, BBNP, RG 79, NA.

felt. His subsequent report would provide the impetus that officially began the movement for Big Bend National Park.[24]

In 1933 Arno B. Cammerer had succeeded Albright as the new Director of the Park Service. Cammerer held reservations about the Big Bend project. "If we could be assured," the Director wrote in the spring of 1934, "that there was enough federal land in the Big Bend country to establish such a park, and it were further investigated for facts as to wildlife, and how to take care of visitors (water supply, camping space, etc.) I would feel that there is a better prospect there than in the Guadalupes."[25]

Events accelerated in April and May 1934 to eliminate Cammerer's doubts. The CCC camp that Representative Thomason had announced in June 1933 finally opened in May 1934. The camp was established in the Chisos Basin after a party led by E. E. Townsend had discovered water there on April 16.[26] The Park Service completed the preliminary wildlife survey on April 18. The study recommended that "from the wildlife point of view" the Big Bend area "is of national parks caliber."[27] In his report Toll had partially quieted the Director's concern about land acquisition when he suggested that the remaining private holdings could be purchased for one to five dollars an acre. Persuaded by the rapid developments in the Big Bend movement, Cammerer approved the proposed national park on May 1, 1934.[28] The next step was to get Secretary of the Interior Harold Ickes's endorsement, after which the Park Service could begin drafting congressional legislation.

---

24. Robert Shankland, *Steve Mather of the National Parks* (3rd ed.; New York: Alfred A. Knopf, 1970), pp. 247–248; Albert Nelson Marquis, ed., *Who's Who in America 1936–1937* (Chicago: The A. N. Marquis Co., 1936), p. 2430; Obituary in *Trail and Timberline*, No. 209 (March–April, 1936), pp. 27–28.

25. U. S. Department of Interior, *Annual Report of the Secretary of the Interior, for the fiscal year ended June 30, 1933* (Washington, D. C.: Government Printing Office, 1933), p. 153; Cammerer memorandum to Arthur E. Demaray, Wirth, and Harold C. Bryant, April 2, 1934, File 0-32, Part I, BBNP, RG 79, NA.

26. Casey, "The Big Bend National Park," chapter three.

27. Ben H. Thompson to Director, NPS, April 18, 1934, File 207, BBNP, RG 79, NA.

28. "Report on the Proposed Big Bend National Park," March 3, 1934, File 207, BBNP, RG 79, NA; "Review of Proposed Big Bend National Park," May 1, 1934, File 0-32, Part I, BBNP, RG 79, NA.

In the summer of 1934 Cammerer authorized an interdepartmental investigation of Big Bend to determine highways, camp sites, and other necessary developments. Also, the study was to provide a guideline for future projects to be undertaken by the CCC workers. In addition, the information gathered was to be presented to the Secretary of the Interior who would determine if the Big Bend project should be presented to Congress. Herbert Maier, the district officer of the CCC and an employee of the NPS, did not complete the report until the following January.[29] It noted that if Mexico were to establish a sister park adjacent to Big Bend's boundary on the Rio Grande the two areas would constitute an international park which "would create ties of kindly sentiment that would multiply and become stronger between the Mexican and American peoples, now almost unknown to each other."[30]

The Maier report also discussed in detail the matter of land ownership and acquisition. The boundaries of the park had been estimated to comprise about 1,500,000 acres. Of this total, the Texas State Parks Board owned 1,640 acres in fee simple title, while 90,000 acres had been gained by the TSPB through tax forfeitures. The State Permanent School Fund held the mineral rights to these 90,000 acres, along with outright ownership of an additional 150,000 acres. Private individuals held 1,250,000 acres, and 6,000 unpurchasable acres belonged to quicksilver mining companies.[31]

The report recognized the complications involved in such land purchases, especially the matter of mineral rights. A national park cannot be guaranteed for future generations if there existed the possibility, for instance, of core mining within its boundaries. Although Texas insisted on retaining the mineral rights, Maier optimistically hoped that these "might be contributed to a national park project by the State Legislature."[32]

Another major hurdle involved the 150,000 acres controlled by

---

29. W. G. Carnes to L. I. Hewes, May 4, 1934, File O-32, Part I, BBNP, RG 79, NA; Maier to Wirth, December 22, 1934, File O-32, Part I, BBNP, RG 79, NA.

30. "Report of the Big Bend Area, Texas," January, 1935, File 207, BBNP, RG 79, NA.

31. *Ibid.*

32. *Ibid.* In 1939, the 46th Legislature released the mineral rights.

the Texas Permanent School Fund. In 1933 the state legislature had given the surface rights to the Texas State Parks Board for a consideration of one cent per acre but the state attorney general later ruled that the transaction constituted a gift rather than a purchase and that the land still belonged to the School Fund. Maier's report suggested that a price of twenty-five cents an acre would make the transfer constitutional and therefore acceptable to the attorney general.[33]

The private lands, on the other hand, could be acquired through tax forfeitures and purchases. These holdings were predominantly low grade grazing lands forty to fifty acres of which were required to sustain a single cow. These submarginal lands were worth from three to five dollars an acre. Overall, the Maier report presented the prospects for a speedy land acquisition program and the likelihood of the early development of Big Bend National Park.[34]

Events began to move rapidly after Maier's study became available. Representative Thomason, a convert to the Big Bend cause since a tour of the area in November 1933, anxiously awaited the chance to introduce a bill in the House for the creation of the park. However, Conrad Wirth of the NPS advised him to wait until Secretary of the Interior Harold Ickes could approve the proposal since this would put any legislative action for the park in a more advantageous position. Ickes acted favorably on February 5, 1935 and Wirth began working with Thomason for appropriate legislation.[35]

The suggestion of an international park brought the Big Bend project to the attention of President Roosevelt and increased national awareness of the region. Senator Morris Sheppard introduced the idea in a letter to Roosevelt on February 16, 1935. Three days later Roosevelt asked Ickes for a report on Sheppard's request for a national and international park. Ickes then sent the President Maier's report and recommended that an invitation be extended to the Mexican government to cooperate with the United States in the

---

33. *Ibid.*

34. *Ibid.*; *Vernon's Texas Statutes 1948*, Art. 6077c.

35. Madison, *The Big Bend Country*, p. 232; Casey, "The Big Bend National Park," p. 37; Thomason to Townsend, January 28, 1935, Box A-1, Bastrop SPW; G. A. Moskey memorandum to Wirth, Hillory Tolson, and Demaray, February 8, 1935, File 0-32, Part I, BBNP, RG 79, NA.

establishment of such a project.[36]

Legislation for Big Bend National Park then proceeded rapidly. On March 4, 1935 Congressman Thomason introduced House Resolution 6373, and on the same day Senators Sheppard and Tom Connally submitted Senate Bill 2131. Sheppard had several letters printed into the *Congressional Record* which stressed the international aspect of the proposed park. The Big Bend project received another boost when the Attorney General of Texas ruled that one cent per acre would be sufficient payment by the Texas State Parks Board to the Permanent Free School Fund for its 150,000 acres in the Big Bend country. The new decision found a penny an acre fair compensation because the School Fund had obtained the mineral rights to lands acquired through tax forfeitures which the Fund, prior to the passage of the Big Bend State Park Act in 1933, had not held. Although this would become the basis for later controversy, it now meant that the Parks Board would soon hold 241,640 acres, or about one-quarter of the estimated necessary amount.[37]

As the legislation at the national level moved quickly through the proper channels with virtually no opposition, popular support for the measure in Texas ran high. Particularly interested were the citizens of Alpine and the surrounding vicinity who viewed the park as a great economic boost to a depressed region. In fact, of the three major park projects in 1935—Olympic in Washington, Kings Canyon in California, and Big Bend—only the Texas project would pass without serious local and congressional opposition. Accordingly, action came on June 20, 1935 and Texas finally had its first national park, at least on paper. The act stipulated that before Big Bend National Park could be established, Texas had to present to the

---

36. Sheppard to the President, February 16, 1935, File 0-32, Part I, BBNP, RG 79, NA; Roosevelt memorandum to the Secretary of the Interior and the Secretary of State, February 19, 1935, File 0-32, Part I, BBNP, RG 79, NA; Ickes to the Secretary of State, March 8, 1935, File 0-32, Part I, BBNP, RG 79, NA; Ickes to the President, February 27, 1935, File 0-32, Part I, BBNP, RG 79, NA.

37. One million acres was the new estimated size for Big Bend in the enabling legislation. U. S. Congress, House, H. R. 6373, 74th Cong., 1st sess., 1935, p. 2916; U. S. Congress, Senate, S. B. 2131, 74th Cong., 1st sess., 1935, p. 2822; D. E. Colp to Wirth, March 11, 1935, File 0-32, Part I, BBNP, RG 79, NA; Grady Chandler and William McCraw to Colp, March 6, 1935, File 0-32, Part I, BBNP, RG 79, NA.

federal government title to all of the lands encompassed by the park boundaries.[38]

Over a period of two and one-half years the Big Bend country had risen from obscurity to one of the most publicized places in the Southwest. Individual efforts by E. E. Townsend and Roger Toll had had much to do with the success of the early park movement. Although President Roosevelt's high regard for national parks was well known, it was the idea of an international park that separated Big Bend from the dozens of other proposals. The depression and the New Deal's CCC program had not only brought the Big Bend region to the attention of the NPS but also provided funds, manpower, and a tentative master plan for its development. The depression likewise affected the local citizenry who quickly saw the economic advantages of a national park.

The element that especially made the Big Bend desirable in a realistic sense was the low economic worth of the land, much of which was overgrazed cattle, sheep, and goat pasturage. Unlike most Western states, Texas did not have a vast expanse of federally owned lands from which many of the early national parks were created. Even with the aesthetic, geological, biological, and international values of the Big Bend, the project never would have made it past Director Cammerer if the land's economic worth had been substantially more than a few cents per acre.

---

38. Ross A. Maxwell, "History of Big Bend National Park" (ms), 1952, Big Bend National Park Library; Demaray to Robert P. Allen, May 17, 1935, File 0-32, Part I, BBNP, RG 79, NA; U. S. Congress, Senate, 74th Cong., 1st sess., 1935, pp. 9620, 9818; U. S., *Statutes at Large*, XLIX, Part I, pp. 393-394.

II The Politics of Fund Raising

Texas had to fulfill two major conditions before Big Bend could be established. The 1935 enabling act stipulated that the state must convey title to the park lands to the Secretary of the Interior and cede exclusive jurisdiction over the area to the federal government. It took nearly a decade to accomplish these objectives. Considering that some park projects required scores of years before they attained full national park status, the delay for Big Bend was comparatively short.[1] Nevertheless, it had an adverse effect on the long-range development of the park.

The congressional legislation for Big Bend came at an inopportune time for Texas politics. The state legislature convened in January of each odd-numbered year. The 44th Legislature had just adjourned shortly before Franklin D. Roosevelt signed the Big Bend Act in June 1935. This meant that any state legislation for the park would have to wait until the winter of 1937, unless Governor James V. Allred called the legislature into a special session in the fall. Counting on such a move, the National Park Service surveyed the Big Bend area and drew up boundaries to help the lawmakers determine the size of the appropriation needed to purchase the lands in the park. The Secretary of the Interior then sent Allred a map and a description of the acreage included in the park. Unfortunately the Governor did not call a special session in the fall of 1935 nor throughout the following year.[2]

---

1. An extreme example is Grand Canyon National Park in Arizona. Senator Benjamin Harrison first proposed the area for a park in 1886. It was not established until 1919.

2. Conrad Wirth telegram to Roger Toll, June 29, 1935, File 0-32, Part I, Big Bend National Park, Record Group 79, National Archives Building (here-

Meanwhile, Allred toured the Big Bend area in November 1935. According to E. E. Townsend, who conducted the Governor's party through the park, he "frankly expressed his approval for the project and said he would do everything he could for it."[3] The Governor even suggested that the state legislators visit Big Bend in order to "sell" them on the idea of a national park for Texas.[4] Otherwise, the chief executive took no specific action at the time.[5]

While the executive and legislative branches remained inactive in regard to Big Bend, the Park Service and local boosters prepared to meet what seemed the major obstacle to the establishment of the park—the mineral rights held by the Public School Fund. Texas law guaranteed that these rights belonged to the state's public schools. Park Service policy dictated that national park lands must have fee simple title. In other words, the mineral rights must be vested solely in the owner, the federal government.

Herbert Maier of the NPS talked with School Fund supporters to determine if any possibility for compromise existed. One alternative was for the federal government to accept the land with the mineral rights still reserved to the School Fund and with the understanding that the Secretary of the Interior alone would decide if future mineral development would take place in the park.[6] The school board officials correctly surmised that there would be no mineral exploitation as long as the area was used for park purposes. Consequently, they were prepared to resist any legislation that would

---

after cited as BBNP, RG 79, NA); Wirth telegram to Herbert Evison, June 26, 1935, File 0-32, Part I, BBNP, RG 79, NA; "Report on Field Investigation Together with Recommendations for the Establishment of a Boundary Line for the Big Bend National Park Project," September 9, 1935, File 0-32, Part II, BBNP, RG 79, NA; Charles West to Allred, October 14, 1935, File 0-32, Part II, BBNP, RG 79, NA.

3. Townsend to Herbert Maier, November 29, 1935, File 0-32, Part II, BBNP, RG 79, NA.

4. *Ibid.*

5. Alexander Brooks memorandum to G. A. Moskey, March 11, 1936, File 0-32, Part III, BBNP, RG 79, NA; Wirth to Gerald Mann, February 11, 1936, File 0-32, Part III, BBNP, RG 79, NA.

6. Regional Officer, Region III to Arno B. Cammerer, November 16, 1936, File 0-32, Part III, BBNP, RG 79, NA; Maier to Wirth, September 13, 1935, File 0-32, Part II, BBNP, RG 79, NA; Maier to Townsend, September 11, 1935, File 0-32, Part II, BBNP, RG 79, NA.

threaten the School Fund.[7]

The Park Service adopted a two-pronged approach to overcome opposition. First, the agency hoped to convince its opponents that little mineral wealth could be found in the Big Bend area. Secondly, it planned to demonstrate that revenue from tourists' dollars from travel to a national park would bring the state's public schools much more than minimal or non-existent mineral resources. The chief geologist for Humble Oil and Refining Company told a NPS scientist that Big Bend contained "possible" but not "probable" oil deposits. Unfortunately, when the 45th Legislature convened in January 1937, the Park Service had not had sufficient time to conduct a thorough investigation. On the brighter side, it appeared the NPS had won its argument regarding the economic advantages of a national park when the Executive Committee of the State Teachers Association in October 1936 endorsed Big Bend as economically and educationally beneficial to the school children of Texas. One positive factor noted was the increased revenues from the gasoline tax. But opposition remained, and Ben F. Tisinger, president of the State Board of Education, emphasized to Herbert Maier on the eve of the legislative session that his organization still advocated the retention by the School Fund of mineral rights in the Big Bend.[8]

Prior to the meeting of the 45th Legislature, the Director of the NPS, Arno B. Cammerer, met in Austin with Maier, Townsend, and Lieutenant Governor Woodul to discuss an appropriation bill for Big Bend National Park. Woodul concurred with Cammerer's suggestion that $1.4 million would be adequate for acquiring the park lands. When the matter of the school lands came up, the Director said the NPS would accept certain mineral reservations, subject to the approval of the Secretary of the Interior. Although Cammerer's statement hinted at compromise, the Park Service still held to the

---

7. Ben F. Tisinger telegram to Senator Morris Sheppard, February 14, 1936, File 0-32, Part III, BBNP, RG 79, NA; Tisinger to Sheppard, February 15, 1936, File 0-32, Part III, BBNP, RG 79, NA; J. O. Guleke and Members of the Texas Board of Education to Sheppard, February 21, 1936, File 0-32, Part III, BBNP, RG 79, NA.

8. L. T. Burrow to Carroll H. Wegemann, September 19, 1935, File 0-32, Part II, BBNP, RG 79, NA; Wegemann to Earl Trager, September 25, 1935, File 0-32, Part II, BBNP, RG 79, NA; Alpine *Avalanche*, October 2, 1936; Maier to Cammerer, January 4, 1937, File 0-32, Part IV, BBNP, RG 79, NA.

original position of fee simple title. Or, if the lands were delivered with reservations, no development of the mineral resources would take place as long as the area was utilized for park purposes.9

Another obstacle to Big Bend emerged when the legislative session began in January. Governor Allred opposed any measures which required additional taxation because of the state's $15,000,000 deficit in the general fund.10 Yet, even against the opposition of the School Fund supporters and a parsimonious governor, the Park Service began to work with H. L. Winfield in the Senate and Coke R. Stevenson in the House to draw up an appropriation bill for land acquisition in the proposed Big Bend National Park.

The bill was prepared in the state attorney general's office and was scheduled for introduction in both houses late in February 1937. The legislation provided for the complete surrender of the School Fund's mineral rights to the federal government after receiving adequate compensation. Another provision established a commission which would direct the land acquisition and make adjustments between the demands of the School Fund and the Secretary of the Interior. Included on the commission were representatives from the State Board of Education as well as other state officials.11

The day before introducing the park appropriation bill, Coke Stevenson issued a press release extolling the economic benefits that Big Bend would bring to Texas. He pointed out that travel agencies estimated in 1936 that the average tourist in America spent five dollars per day. If 50,000 came to Big Bend during the year and spent four extra days in the state, that would produce an additional income of $1,000,000. Stevenson's figures actually were conservative, since more than 150,000 had visited Carlsbad Caverns in 1936 and over 500,000 had gone to Rocky Mountain National Park. Texas would also gain the revenue from federal maintenance, development, and

---

9. Maier to Director, NPS, November 13, 1936, File 0-32, Part III, BBNP, RG 79, NA; Cammerer telegram to Maier, November 19, 1936, File 0-32, Part III, BBNP, RG 79, NA; Arthur Demaray telegram to Maier, January 6, 1937, File 0-32, Part IV, BBNP, RG 79, NA.

10. Maier to Director, NPS, January 27, 1937, File 0-32, Part IV, BBNP, RG 79, NA; Maier to Director, NPS, January 28, 1937, File 0-32, Part IV, BBNP, RG 79, NA.

11. Maier to Director, NPS, attention of Moskey, February 18, 1937, File 0-32, Part IV, BBNP, RG 79, NA; Fort Worth *Star-Telegram*, March 3, 1937.

payrolls. Stevenson closed on the note that the Texas Centennial celebrations in Dallas and Fort Worth had attracted thousands of visitors to the Lone Star State, but only for a temporary show. Big Bend, on the other hand, represented a "permanent exposition."[12] Several newspapers supported the state legislator's position, including the influential Fort Worth *Star-Telegram*.[13]

By the end of March committees in both houses had reported favorably on an appropriation bill for $2,000,000 to purchase approximately 1,000,000 acres for a national park in the Big Bend region of Texas. Winfield introduced the bill first in the Senate, since park backers expected possible opposition from this body because of its alliance with the state's large industries. They would receive the brunt of the taxation required for the Big Bend appropriation. If the legislation could get past the Senate, passage in the House was considered a certainty.[14]

The Senate objected to several features of the bill, particularly the $2,000,000 appropriation and the independent commission in charge of land acquisition. Nevertheless, it passed the legislation in late April but cut the amount to $750,000. With the session almost over, it seemed doubtful if the measure carried as a separate bill there would be time for passage in the House before the legislature adjourned on May 11. To guarantee the bill's success, however, Representative Stevenson tacked it on to the appropriation for the general revenue fund. He also offered two amendments to appease the Senate by reducing the House's suggested appropriation of $2,000,000 to $750,000 and by turning over the administration of the land purchase program to the Texas State Parks Board. As a final conciliatory move in behalf of the School Fund, Representative Alf Roark introduced an amendment which would allow the public schools to keep their mineral rights. The bill then went to conference committee where it was approved and sent to Governor Allred.[15]

The Governor had until June 11 to make up his mind, but what

---

12. Stevenson's Press Release, February 21, 1937, File 0–32, Part IV, BBNP, RG 79, NA.

13. Fort Worth *Star-Telegram*, February 20, 1937.

14. Maier to Director, NPS, attention of Wirth, March 27, 1937, File 0–32, Part IV, BBNP, RG 79, NA.

15. Austin *Dispatch*, May 17, 1937.

he would do with the bill remained very much in doubt. He still publicly expressed his support for Big Bend, but campaign commitments against additional appropriation measures placed him in an awkward position. Even so, Allred had previously told park backers that if the appropriation bill passed both houses, he would not veto it.[16]

During the interim, the NPS and other park backers used various means to persuade Allred. It was rumored that the Governor desired a newly created federal judgeship in east Texas when his term ended. One Park Service official suggested that United States Representative Sam Rayburn and Senator Morris Sheppard, both supporters of Big Bend National Park and influential in selecting federal judges for the state, should call Allred and "mention the two things in one breath."[17] Another complication regarding a veto was the possibility of upsetting the work accomplished toward the creation of the international park. Herbert Maier contacted the Mexican officials responsible for the project in their country. They in turn notified the American ambassador's office of their approval of the $750,000 appropriation bill. Ambassador Josephus Daniels then relayed the message to Allred. Pro-Big Bend groups besieged the Governor's office daily and Director Cammerer stressed the social and economic advantages of a national park for Texas, observing that Big Bend would repay the legislature's appropriation "one-hundred fold." But all these efforts failed when Allred vetoed the measure.[18]

The Governor gave several reasons for his action. He regarded the appropriation as insufficient for the purchase of all the Big Bend land and that the unsold private portions would then increase in value. Also, he felt that the federal government probably would not accept the acres with the mineral rights still in the possession of

---

16. Maier to Director, NPS, attention of Wirth, May 1, 1937, File O-32, Part IV, BBNP, RG 79, NA; Maier to Director, NPS, attention of Wirth, April 16, 1937, File O-32, Part IV, BBNP, RG 79, NA.

17. Maier to Director, NPS, attention of Wirth, May 31, 1937, File O-32, Part IV, BBNP, RG 79, NA.

18. Maier to Departmento Forestal, Gaza y Pesca, attention of Daniel F. Galicia or Juan Zinser, May 26, 1937, File O-32, Part IV, BBNP, RG 79, NA; M. A. de Quevedo to Pierre del Boal June 4, 1937, File O-32, Part IV, BBNP, RG 79, NA; Boal telegram to Daniels, June 5, 1937, File O-32, Part IV, BBNP, RG 79, NA; Cammerer telegram to Allred, June 5, 1937, File O-32, Part IV, BBNP, RG 79, NA.

the School Fund. Moreover, park advocates might later request an additional appropriation to buy the remaining lands and pressure the School Fund to relinquish its rights, especially since the state would already have so much invested in Big Bend. In addition, Allred disliked the idea of tying such a large appropriation bill to the general revenue fund and he also believed that the special appropriation would put too much of a strain on the already depleted treasury.[19]

There were several contradictions in Allred's arguments. On the one hand, he called for the complete purchase of Big Bend, yet on the other he opposed appropriation measures which would increase taxes. Also, his position on the mineral rights issue did not really indicate wholehearted support for a national park. Allred's comment about the need for a separate bill for Big Bend was interesting, because if his advice had been followed, there would not even have been a bill to veto. One thing can be said in the Governor's favor, however—his public statements provided publicity for the park.

The veto initiated a determined effort by various West Texans to raise the necessary funds to acquire the Big Bend lands. An editorial in the Fort Worth *Star-Telegram* called for one million Texans to give one dollar each toward the purchase of Big Bend acres. The idea was inspired by the citizens of Virginia who previously had raised approximately $1,000,000 for the acquisition of Shenandoah National Park. Herbert Maier asked the managing editor, James R. Record, if his newspaper would sponsor the fund raising campaign. Horace Morelock, in behalf of the Local Park Committee of the Alpine Chamber of Commerce, also made a strong appeal to the *Star-Telegram*.[20]

Other newspapers throughout the state joined in publicizing Big Bend, but the *Star-Telegram* led the fund raising activities among

---

19. *Legislative Messages of Governor James V. Allred, 1935-1939*, Big Bend National Park Library (hereafter cited as BBNP Lib); Allred to Daniels, June 15, 1937, File 0-32, Part IV, BBNP, RG 79, NA; Leo McClatchy, "Big Bend Campaign." (ms), August 18, 1937, File 0-32, Part IV, BBNP, RG 79, NA.

20. Fort Worth *Star-Telegram*, June 11, 1937; Maier to Record, July 13, 1937, Amon Carter Museum (hereafter cited as ACM); Morelock to Fort Worth *Star-Telegram*, June 12, 1937, File 0-32, Part IV, BBNP, RG 79, NA; J. M. North to Morelock, June 21, 1937, File 0-32, Part IV, BBNP, RG 79, NA; Maier to Director, NPS, attention of Wirth, July 13, 1937, File 0-32, Part IV, BBNP, RG 79, NA.

Texas dailies. A regular feature in the Fort Worth paper was a list of names and amounts each donor had given, often accompanied by a story about the park area. One edition carried a picture of Governor Allred contributing a dollar to the campaign. Another article encouraged school children to give their nickels and dimes. A fifth grade class from Marfa, Texas responded with one dollar which they had won for their parents's perfect attendance at a PTA meeting. Their teacher matched the amount. On a larger scale, the city of San Angelo raised $1,300 in a drive conducted by the Junior Chamber of Commerce.[21] Although the *Star-Telegram* gave the Big Bend a generous amount of free publicity and also served as a collector for some of the funds acquired, it was not the prime mover behind the subscription campaign.

The Brewster County and Alpine Chambers of Commerce under the able leadership of Dom Adams, Jim Casner, and Horace Morelock provided the nucleus for a state-wide organization for the park movement. Operations began in mid-July 1937 when they asked each of the 254 counties in the state to set up local park committees of the leading businessmen, educators, and public officials.[22]

The most active and immodest member of the West Texas campaign was Morelock, chairman of the Local Park Committee and president of Sul Ross State Teachers College in Alpine. He admitted spending almost half his time trying to convince the people of Texas of the worth of the Big Bend project. Morelock wrote twenty to thirty letters per day and traveled thousands of miles to talk with those who might be interested in the project, including a substantial number of representatives of oil, railroads, and other major industries. His endeavors were not wholly unselfish, for he regarded Big Bend National Park as an extension of the Sul Ross campus, as well as a stimulus for the community of Alpine.[23]

Unfortunately, Morelock's enthusiasm and the efforts of the Brewster County and Alpine Chambers of Commerce, the Local Park

---

21. Fort Worth *Star-Telegram*, July 25, 1937; October 3, 1937; October 9, 1937; September 8, 1937; September 16, 1937.

22. Dallas *Morning News*, July 25, 1937; El Paso *Times* (date obscured), File 0-32, Part V, BBNP, RG 79, NA.

23. Morelock to Harold Ickes, October 25, 1937, File 0-32, Part V, BBNP, RG 79, NA.

Committees, and the Fort Worth *Star-Telegram* were insufficient. After four months of intense campaigning, the amount collected was approximately $50,000, far short of the $1,000,000 goal.[24]

One casualty of the unsuccessful campaign was the CCC camp in the Chisos Mountains. The camp enrollees had built twenty miles of roads, trails, and other projects. All told, the federal government had spent $323,680 on improvements. Yet without a guarantee that title to the lands would be transferred to the Department of the Interior, the NPS could not develop the park site further. The Park Service had expressed encouragement at the initial results of the fund raising drive when it began in July. But when the campaign proved ineffectual and the 45th Legislature in a called session that fall failed to appropriate any funds for land purchase, the CCC camp was subsequently abandoned on December 15, 1937. Park advocates vigorously protested the decision. Their only consolation was Conrad Wirth's promise to Ewing Thomason that the Park Service hoped to reoccupy Big Bend at a later date, at which time three of four CCC camps would be opened.[25]

The called session in the fall of 1937 at least accomplished something for Big Bend. Both houses overwhelmingly passed legislation that officially recognized the national park, approved its boundaries as recommended by the Secretary of the Interior, and authorized the Texas State Parks Board to receive donations of land and money. The bill also granted the Board the power of eminent domain. Allred signed the measure and at long last part of the bureaucratic and legal machinery necessary for the establishment of Big Bend National Park had been created. Instead of a haphazard organizational structure, as in the case of the Local Park Committees, all contributions would eventually come to the State Parks Board which in turn would purchase the lands and transfer them to the federal government.[26] Still

---

24. Maier telegram to Director, NPS, attention of Fred T. Johnston, November 20, 1937, File 0–32, Part V, BBNP, RG 79, NA.

25. Houston *Chronicle*, July 25, 1937; Fort Worth *Star-Telegram*, September 1, 1937; NPS Press Release, December 11, 1937, File 0–32, Part V, BBNP, RG 79, NA; Fort Worth *Star-Telegram*, November 20, 1937; Wirth to Thomason, November 10, 1937, File 0–32, Part V, BBNP, RG 79, NA; Fort Worth *Star-Telegram*, November 25, 1937.

26. Adams to Cammerer, June 18, 1937, File 0–32, Part IV, BBNP, RG 79, NA; Johnston to Regional Director, Region III, June 25, 1937, File 0–32, Part

unresolved was how to obtain the relatively large sum of $1,000,000 since the subscription campaign had fared so poorly.

An appropriation was out of the question because the legislature would not convene again until the winter of 1939. After considering several other alternatives, in January 1938 Big Bend supporters returned to the original idea of a popular subscription campaign. The Local Park Committees and the State Parks Board reorganized, and a temporary Executive Committee was appointed to formulate policy. Selected to this body were several of the state's wealthiest and most politically powerful citizens, including Amon Carter, Sr. The publisher of the Fort Worth *Star-Telegram* was chosen chairman by a unanimous vote of the committee members because of his organizing abilities and the excellent coverage his newspaper had given Big Bend.[27]

Allred summoned the interim Executive Committee to Austin in the spring of 1938, along with 150 prominent Texans to boost the revived park project. From this group he appointed twenty-six members to the permanent Executive Committee of a newly created organization, the Texas Big Bend Park Association. Its purpose was to publicize Big Bend National Park and raise funds for land acquisition. Amon Carter was retained as chairman. H. W. Morelock became vice chairman, and the Governor honorary president. Carter then spoke of the advantages of tourism for the Lone Star State and confidently predicted the success of the popular subscription campaign. All agreed that the major stumbling block for the successful completion of the drive was that old nemesis, mineral rights. Indeed, the School Fund held one-sixteenth royalty on 343,354 acres owned by individuals and full royalty on 139,168 acres in the state's possession. The Executive Committee did not dwell on this issue for fear

---

IV, BBNP, RG 79, NA; Demaray to Daniels, July 2, 1937, File 0-32, Part IV, BBNP, RG 79, NA; Fort Worth *Star-Telegram*, September 4, 1937; Cammerer memorandum to Ickes, August 8, 1937, File 0-32, Part IV, BBNP, RG 79, NA; *Vernon's Texas Statutes 1948*, Art. 6077c; Alpine *Avalanche*, November 5, 1937.

27. Morelock to Carter, March 10, 1938, File 0-32, Part V, BBNP, RG 79, NA. The other members of the temporary Executive Committee were: Wendell Mayes, Brownwood; J. E. Josey, Houston; W. B. Tuttle, San Antonio; John W. Carpenter, Dallas; Jesse H. Jones, Houston; C. H. Bassett, El Paso; Gus Taylor, Tyler; W. L. Moody, III, Galveston; Mrs. Richard J. Turrentine, Denton; Mrs. M. A. Taylor, Bonham; James R. Record, Fort Worth; John E. King, Dallas; Luther Stark, Beaumont; H. W. Morelock, Alpine.

that it would dampen enthusiasm for the fund drive.[28]

The Big Bend Park Association appeared off to a good start when Carter subscribed $5,000 to a working fund to cover rent for a headquarters office and additional campaign expenses. Another $20,000 was pledged by other committee members. Adrian Wychgel of the firm Adrian Wychgel and Associates, an institutional finance organization, talked to the group about his company's success at raising almost $2,000,000 for Mammoth Cave and Shenandoah National Parks in Kentucky and Virginia. Wychgel assured Allred that "very little, if any, money would have to be appropriated by the State." At both Mammoth Cave and Shenandoah he had achieved his goal in less than six months. Wychgel wanted to begin the campaign immediately and forecast a successful conclusion to the drive by November 1938.[29]

The Big Bend Park Association finally retained the Wychgel firm, but fund raising efforts still had not begun in full force by the opening of the 46th Legislative session. Meanwhile, the Texas press kept Big Bend constantly before the public and contributions continually trickled in. The Park Association drive remained stymied because the directors had not honored their pledges to the working fund, as only $15,500 had been received of the necessary $25,000. According to Carter, the Big Bend Park Association could not proceed with a large scale campaign until the working fund was paid in full.[30]

As it became more and more apparent throughout the summer and fall of 1938 that the Big Bend Park Association would not inaugurate its fund raising campaign, the Park Service looked toward the approaching regular legislative session. In June, Ewing Thomason met in Washington with the NPS hierarchy. The topics of discussion revolved about the school lands and the procedure to follow concerning another bill for Big Bend. Thomason felt the park's for-

---

28. Fort Worth *Star-Telegram*, May 24, 1938; Maier to Director, NPS, May 28, 1938, File 0–32, Part VII, BBNP, RG 79, NA. The Permanent Executive Committee eventually grew to a membership of fifty directors by 1941.

29. Minutes of Meeting of the Executive Board, Texas Big Bend Park Association, May 23, 1938, ACM; Wychgel to Allred, May 28, 1938, Box A-7, Bastrop State Park Warehouse, Bastrop, Texas.

30. Maier memorandum to Director, NPS, November 22, 1938, File 0–32, Part VI, BBNP, RG 79, NA.

tunes would change for the better at the next session, since Texas would have a different governor and a large number of new faces in the 46th Legislature.[31]

The Governor-elect, W. Lee "Pappy" O'Daniel would prove to be a real friend of the Big Bend movement. From his vacation headquarters in Galveston, he expressed best wishes for the fund raising drive. Park backers in Brewster County even suggested that the Governor-elect use the same tactics to raise money for the Big Bend that he had utilized so successfully in his victorious campaign. O'Daniel had been a well-known flour salesman and radio entertainer before entering politics. During the spring Democratic primary, he had toured the state with his daughter Molly, sons Mike and Pat, and his Hillbilly Band. Contributions poured in and his campaign became one of the most colorful in Texas political history. He eventually won a decisive victory over a field of twelve contenders.[32]

In the fall of 1938 O'Daniel visited the national park site and Herbert Maier found him reasonably impressed. The Governor-elect later gave Arthur Demaray, Acting Director of the NPS, his unqualified support for Big Bend and promised to "do everything possible for the project."[33]

One positive aspect of the new administration was the Lieutenant Governor, Coke Stevenson, who had introduced the unsuccessful appropriation bill before the legislature in 1937. Stevenson would again work on the Big Bend legislation during the forthcoming 1939 session with H. L. Winfield, now a member of the powerful Banking and Finance Committee. Their legislation did not originally include a request for funds, but a nominal appropriation of $1,000 was added to the bill to give it priority in the committee hearings

---

31. Thomason to Morelock, July 1, 1938, File O-32, Part VII, BBNP, RG 79, NA; Cammerer memorandum to Maier and the Files, July 11, 1938, File O-32, Part VII, BBNP, RG 79, NA.

32. Galveston *News*, August 8, 1938; Dallas *Morning News*, September 9, 1938; San Antonio *Light*, August 15, 1938; O'Daniel received 573,166 votes out of 1,114,885 cast. See *Texas Almanac, 1956-1957* (Dallas: The Dallas Morning News, 1955), p. 73.

33. Goose Creek *Sun*, October 19, 1938; Maier memorandum to Director, NPS, November 22, 1938, File O-32, Part VI, BBNP RG 79, NA; O'Daniel to Demaray, December 20, 1938, File O-32, Part VI, BBNP, RG 79, NA.

and on the floor of the Senate and House.[34]

Amon Carter gave explicit instructions that the Big Bend measure should carry no major appropriation. Explanations for Carter's position varied from speculation that he expected a large contribution from a private donor, to rumors that he did not want to obligate himself to the new governor. The most likely reason, however, was that Carter feared a substantial appropriation bill would upset the private subscription campaign. In fact, the Big Bend Park Association hoped to complete the fund raising drive by the end of the 1939 legislative session.[35]

The Winfield Senate Bill Number 123 granted the Texas State Parks Board the right of public domain as well as the power to acquire lands for the park through purchase, condemnation, or as donations. The maximum price per acre of private land exclusive of improvements was set at two dollars. These provisions generally were amplifications of the act passed at the called session in the fall of 1937 with two significant additions—sections III and IV. Section III transferred the unsold School Fund lands to the state in fee simple title for park purposes at a price of one dollar per acre to be paid from the general fund. The School Fund also held the mineral rights on the privately owned lands and section IV authorized the transfer of these rights to the state for a consideration of fifty cents an acre.[36]

O'Daniel spoke of the Winfield bill as "an investment which would pay good returns."[37] In a message to the Texas Senate he declared that an emergency existed in the Big Bend country and that unless the 46th Legislature acted immediately on the pending bill, the unauthorized collection of archaeological and geological treasures, as well as other acts of vandalism, would leave the state with only the picked-clean skeleton of what had once been a superlative national park site. The Governor was exuberant over Big Bend and

---

34. Maier memorandum to Director, NPS, January 24, 1939, File O-32, Part VI, BBNP, RG 79, NA; Fort Worth *Star-Telegram*, April 5, 1939.

35. *Ibid.*; Maier to Winfield, January 24, 1939, File O-32, Part VI, BBNP, RG 79, NA.

36. Draft of SB 123, File O-32, Part VI, BBNP, RG 79, NA; San Antonio *Express*, March 4, 1939. Chapter 3 deals specifically with the land acquisition program for Big Bend National Park.

37. Austin *Times*, March 7, 1939.

called it "this great 'GIFT OF GOD' to Texas and our nation." He referred to the Chisos Range as "the most rugged mountains in the world" and the Big Bend landscape as "the most gorgeous on the continent." The Governor recounted the economic advantages that would accrue to the state with a national park and inserted a letter from Franklin D. Roosevelt in his message to the legislature in which the President asked for the establishment of Big Bend. The Governor concluded his remarks by requesting the legislature to give the park bill "IMMEDIATE ATTENTION."[38]

Governor O'Daniel's concern for the park had considerable effect on the 46th Legislature. The Senate passed the Winfield bill unanimously. Representative Jeff Stinson tried to amend it in the House to reserve the School Fund's mineral rights, arguing that Big Bend might contain valuable deposits of oil and quicksilver. Representative Albert R. Cauthorn, who had introduced Winfield's bill in the House, successfully countered Stinson's argument when he produced data that showed Big Bend National Park would generate revenues of $3,500,000 from tourist travel. He also assured the School Fund supporters that in the event the lands were not used for park purposes, the federal government would return them to the state. The House then passed the Big Bend bill by a 109–20 vote and O'Daniel signed it on May 12, 1939. The act was the only triumph of his first administration, since none of his other major bills passed.[39]

Although no funds had been appropriated for land purchase, the Park Service was greatly encouraged over the provision for the transfer in fee simple title to the federal government. The agency consequently reestablished the CCC camp in the Chisos Mountains in the Big Bend. But the lack of an appropriation now meant that the campaign headed by Carter would have to raise $1,500,000, since the value of the land had increased and the School Fund required compensation for relinquishing its mineral rights. However, Carter refused to proceed until the working fund had reached $25,000. He

---

38. *Journal of the Senate of Texas*, 46th Legislature, Reg. sess., March 1, 1939, pp. 476–478. The italics are O'Daniel's.

39. Alpine *Avalanche*, May 2, 1939; Temple *Telegraph*, May 2, 1939; Fort Worth *Star-Telegram*, May 2, 1939; Del Rio *Herald*, April 7, 1939; Texarkana *News*, June 22, 1939.

also felt the business conditions in Texas were not yet stable enough to begin an intensified campaign. Governor O'Daniel soon grew apprehensive that the Big Bend Park Association would not succeed and that the forthcoming 47th Legislature would have to appropriate the money necessary for the acquisition of park lands, if it was to be purchased at all.[40]

The Big Bend Park Association never did open its full-scale campaign. Most of the blame belonged to the Executive Committee chairman, Amon Carter, Sr., but some of the other committee members also were at fault. They not only failed to honor their pledges, but refused to commit themselves wholeheartedly to the drive because of a strong dislike for the chairman. Several regarded Carter as an opportunist who would "reap all the credit" for the establishment of Big Bend, yet do very little of the actual work. Carter's inaccessibility and disdain for correspondence likewise hindered his effectiveness.[41]

The chairman meanwhile blamed the deteriorating political and military situation in Europe and Asia, poor business conditions for Texas's large industries, and finally, the war hysteria of the 1940s. The publisher had hoped to raise the money chiefly from corporations and philanthropic organizations, which partly explains his reluctance to push the fund raising effort when conditions did not seem right for the large giver. Humble Oil Company, for example, the richest corporation in Texas, would pledge only a thousand dollars.[42]

---

40. Wirth telegram to Regional Director, Region III, May 19, 1939, File O-32, Part VI, BBNP, RG 79, NA; NPS Press Release, June 30, 1939, File 501-03, Part II, BBNP, RG 79, NA; Vernon *Record*, July 3, 1939; Fort Worth *Star-Telegram*, May 14, 1939; Audit of the Texas Big Bend Park Association Working Fund, June 12, 1941, ACM. This audit showed pledges of $26,907.90 but $3,057.91 were never paid. Thus the working fund never did reach $25,000. Fort Worth *Star-Telegram*, May 16, 1941; Maier memorandum to Director, NPS, October 19, 1939, File O-32, Part VII, BBNP, RG 79, NA; Hillory Tolson memorandum to Johnston, November 10, 1939, File O-32, Part VII, BBNP, RG 79, NA; Ben H. Thompson memorandum to Wirth, January 5, 1940, File O-32, Part VIII, BBNP, RG 79, NA.

41. Maier memorandum to Director, NPS, November 22, 1938. File O-32, Part VI, BBNP, RG 79, NA; Tolson memorandum to Johnston, November 10, 1939, File O-32, Part VII, BBNP, RG 79, NA; Maxwell memorandum to Regional Director, Region III, July 26, 1948, File 610, BBNP, RG 79, NA.

42. Maier memorandum to Director, NPS, May 13, 1939, File O-32, Part

All factors considered, Amon Carter and the Texas Big Bend Park Association probably did more to hinder than to help the project. After three years the Carter committee had raised only $9,582.93. In addition, some Texas cities and assorted organizations contributed directly to the Texas State Parks Board so that by the fall of 1940 an estimated $50–100,000 had been raised, far short of the $1,500,000 needed for land purchases.[43]

Since the Big Bend enabling act had forbidden the use of federal funds for land acquisition,[44] it was obvious by now that if Texas were ever to have a national park, the only alternative was through a state appropriation. Accordingly, Governor O'Daniel asked the 47th Legislature in his opening address in January 1941 to make provisions for land acquisition funds.[45] The Park Service also made preparation to help, and its lobbyist, E. E. Townsend, would remain at the capital at his own expense to work for the passage of an appropriation bill. Minor R. Tillotson, Regional Director for the NPS in the Southwest, testified before the House Appropriations Committee on the increased tourist travel that would result from the creation of the Big Bend Park. In addition, Tillotson prepared data on the economic benefits derived from national parks for Governor O'Daniel's weekly radio broadcasts. On March 19, the House Committee reported favorably on the Big Bend appropriation bill by an 11–3 vote, the Senate Finance Committee having previously

---

VI, BBNP, RG 79, NA; Milton McColm memorandum to Director, NPS, August 13, 1940, File 0–32, Part VIII, BBNP, RG 79, NA; Carter to Members of Executive Committee BBPA, October 22, 1940, File 0–32, Part VIII, BBNP, RG 79, NA; Fort Worth *Star-Telegram*, August 25, 1940.

43. M. R. Tillotson memorandum to Director, NPS, February 27, 1943, File 601, Part I, BBNP, RG 79, NA; Fort Worth *Star-Telegram*, May 16, 1941; McColm telegram to Director, NPS, April 10, 1940, File 0–32, Part VIII, BBNP, RG 79, NA; Maier memorandum to Director, NPS, November 22, 1938, File 0–32, Part VI, BBNP, RG 79, NA. Carter said the land purchase program would commence as soon as the BBPA raised $100,000 through popular subscription (exclusive of the working fund). Since it never began, the figure of $100,000 would be a maximum estimation. See Maier memorandum to Director, NPS, May 13, 1939, File 0–32, Part VI, BBNP, RG 79, NA.

44. A. J. Wirtz to Morelock, August 20, 1940, File 0–32, Part VIII, BBNP, RG 79, NA.

45. Townsend to Tillotson, January 17, 1941, File 0–32, Part VIII, BBNP, RG 79, NA; L. C. Fuller memorandum to Tillotson, January 20, 1941, File 0–32, Part VIII, BBNP, RG 79, NA.

approved the measure unanimously.[46]

When the bill came before the House for discussion, Representative G. C. Morris offered an amendment to reserve the mineral rights for the state. Morris, a strong supporter of the School Fund, observed that the Big Bend area could well become as productive as the East Texas oil fields. But a joint committee of the House and Senate later struck out the amendment. As finally written, the legislation called for an appropriation of $1,500,000. By July 3, 1941 it had passed both houses and was signed into law by the Governor.[47] The appraised value of the lands needed, $1,486,000 including improvements, was well within the limits of the appropriation.[48]

The land purchase program began in earnest almost immediately and proceeded so smoothly that by November 1942 all but 13,316 acres had been acquired. Newton B. Drury, who succeeded Cammerer as Director of the Park Service in 1941, hoped that these private lands could be acquired also. But when it became apparent that much time would elapse, he recommended to the Secretary of the Interior that the acres already purchased be accepted on the condition that the Texas State Parks Board would make every effort possible to complete the land purchase program. The Secretary concurred with Drury's suggestion.[49]

On September 5, 1943 Governor Coke Stevenson presented the land deeds to Minor Tillotson of the Park Service. The Governor had yet to sign the deed of cession of jurisdiction and forward it to the Secretary of the Interior. Before this could take place there first had

---

46. *Ibid.*; Tillotson memorandum to Director, NPS, March 6, 1941, File 0–32, Part VIII, BBNP, RG 79, NA; Tillotson, "The Big Bend National Park as an Asset to the State of Texas" (ms), March 27, 1941, File 0–32, Part VIII, BBNP, RG 79, NA; Tillotson telegram to Director, NPS, March 20, 1941, File 0–32, Part VIII, BBNP, RG 79, NA.

47. John C. Diggs memorandum to Regional Director, Region III, June 9, 1941, File 0–32, Part IX, BBNP, RG 79, NA; Ross Maxwell, "History of Big Bend National Park" (ms), BBNP Lib.

48. Fort Worth *Star-Telegram*, August 8, 1941; Frank Quinn to Tillotson, December 18, 1941, File 0–32, Part IX, BBNP, RG 79, NA.

49. Tillotson memorandum to Director, NPS, November 10, 1942, File 601, Part I, BBNP, RG 79, NA; Carter to Drury, April 15, 1943, File 601, Part I, BBNP, RG 79, NA; Moskey memorandum to Wirth, May 1, 1943, File 601, Part I, BBNP, RG 79, NA; Drury memorandum to Secretary of the Interior, June 7, 1943, File 601, Part II, BBNP, RG 79, NA.

to be a final check made on the land titles, as well as other related matters to be taken care of. These were eventually accomplished and on December 30, 1943 Stevenson signed the deed of cession and chose Amon Carter to deliver it to Harold Ickes. Not content simply to give it to the Secretary of the Interior, Carter insisted that the ceremony also be witnessed by the President in the White House. The difficulty of catching Roosevelt in Washington with a spare moment during this critical war period delayed the ceremony until June 6, 1944. Big Bend gained full national park status six days later.[50]

Carter's failure to deliver the deed for six months caused much consternation among local, state, and national supporters of Big Bend. During this time the development of the park remained at a standstill. The Park Service could not police the area until it had been granted jurisdictional privileges, and, unfortunately, vandals destroyed or damaged many of the park's resources. Carter's *Star-Telegram* does deserve praise for the excellent coverage it provided for the Big Bend Park movement. But its publisher's contribution can best be summed up in the words of a distraught Park Service official who felt the chairman of the fund drive had little interest in Big Bend unless it offered "publicity for himself or for his newspaper."[51]

From 1933 well into 1941 the National Park Service received a total of $218 million for various New Deal programs for its various parks. Over $130 million of this amount went to the Civilian Conservation Corps. Big Bend missed out on most of the progress except for the CCC camp in the Chisos Mountains. Unfortunately the CCC was discontinued in 1942 just when Big Bend was ready to expand through its land purchase program. With America's entry into World War II, the formerly ample NPS appropriations ceased and the neglect of the national parks continued until well after the Korean War. These were key years for Big Bend and it would suf-

---

50. W. Lee O'Daniel filled the senate seat vacated when Morris Sheppard died in 1941. Tolson memorandum to Solicitor General, August 31, 1944, File 601, Part II, BBNP, RG 79, NA; Harry Connelly to Drury, June 11, 1942, File 0-32, Part IX, BBNP, RG 79, NA; Washington *Star*, June 7, 1944.

51. Drury to Carter, March 27, 1944, File 601, Part II, BBNP, RG 79, NA; Drury to Carter, May 24, 1944, File 601, Part II, BBNP, RG 79, NA; Houston *Press*, April 7, 1944; Tillotson memorandum to Director, NPS, January 23, 1945, File 501-04, BBNP, RG 79, NA.

fer from lack of personnel and funds and for almost two decades remained substandard as to roads, visitor facilities, and interpretive programs.[52] Consequently, the physical development of Big Bend did not really reach fruition until the 1960s when Mission 66 finally made available much-needed moneys for improvement and development of all our national parks.

---

52. Robert Shankland, *Steve Mather of the National Parks* (3rd ed.; New York: Alfred A. Knopf, 1970), pp. 306, 311; William C. Everhart, *The National Park Service* (New York: Praeger Publishers, 1972), pp. 33-34; F. Fraser Darling and Noel D. Eichhorn, *Man and Nature in the National Parks* (2nd ed.; Washington, D. C.: The Conservation Foundation, 1969), pp. 26, 40.

III Land Acquisition

A land purchase program was already underway before the Big Bend Enabling Act became law on June 20, 1935. Late in 1934 the National Park Service appointed Everett Ewing Townsend from Alpine project manager to coordinate the classification of the proposed 1,500,000 acres. The predominantly submarginal grazing lands were estimated to be worth from one to five dollars per acre. Townsend, in conjunction with the Texas State Parks Board and the Park Service, would soon lay the foundation for an efficient land purchase program.[1]

Because of the unique status of Texas's public lands, the Park Service followed the procedure for its eastern parks with Big Bend; namely, that the enabling authorization provided for the state to present the land for the parks to the federal government. Also, with Big Bend, as earlier with Appalachian, Isle Royale, and Everglades National Parks, the enabling acts were passed before the exact area was determined. This was done because much of the acreage was privately owned and the difficulty of land purchase would cause numerous revisions of an individual park boundary.[2]

In September 1935 the Park Service recommended boundaries for the proposed Big Bend park. Over the following years several revisions occurred because of the need to conform to surveys and

---

1. Herbert Maier to Conrad Wirth, December 22, 1934, File O-32, Part I, Records of Big Bend National Park, Record Group 79, National Archives Building (hereafter cited as BBNP, RG 79, NA); "Report on the Proposed Big Bend National Park," March 3, 1934, File 207, BBNP, RG 79, NA; "Report of the Big Bend Area, Texas," January, 1935, File 207, BBNP, RG 79, NA.

2. John Ise, *Our National Park Policy: A Critical History* (Baltimore: Johns Hopkins Press, 1961), pp. 376, 380.

to insure that only property absolutely essential for the park was included. None of the changes, however, excluded the four main geographical and scenic features of the area—the Chisos Mountains and Boquillas, Mariscal, and Santa Elena Canyons.[3]

Townsend completed the classification of the Big Bend lands in the fall of 1936. The proposed area for the park at this time comprised approximately 788,682 acres. The state owned nearly one-seventh of this total, while private corporations and individuals held the rest. Through forfeitures and donations, the State Parks Board had fee simple title to only 112,907 acres by May 1941, with nearly 676,000 remaining to be acquired. A private subscription campaign begun in 1937 failed to raise more than a few thousand dollars, but in 1941 the 47th Legislature fortunately appropriated $1,500,000 for acquisition purposes. The amount seemed ample at the time, based on two dollars as the maximum allowed per acre, exclusive of improvements. Meanwhile, the State Parks Board organized the Big Bend Land Department with headquarters in Alpine and appointed Eugene "Shorty" Thompson administrator and E. E. Townsend as his assistant. The appraised value of the land was $1,486,000.[4] The legislative act stipulated that the Big Bend Land Department had only twelve months to purchase the land, otherwise the unexpended funds would revert to the state's general fund.[5] Thompson and Townsend

---

3. "Report on Field Investigation Together with Recommendations for the Establishment of a Boundary Line for the Big Bend National Park Project," September 9, 1935, File 0-32, Part II, BBNP, RG 79, NA; Acting Director, NPS to Director, Geological Survey, March 11, 11936 File 0-32, Part III, BBNP, RG 79, NA; "Status of Approved Land Acquisition Programs," February 8, 1943, File 601, Part II, BBNP, RG 79, NA; Newton B. Drury memorandum to Secretary of the Interior, December 22, 1942, File 601, 0-32, BBNP, RG 79, NA; Eugene Thompson to M. R. Tillotson, August 23, 1943, File 601, Part II, BBNP, RG 79, NA. There were several other boundary revisions between 1949 and 1973. Today the park comprises 708,118.40 acres.

4. Maier to Wirth, October 30, 1936, File 0-32, Part III, BBNP, RG 79, NA; Hillory Tolson memorandum to Director, NPS, February 1, 1939, File 0-32, Part III, BBNP, RG 79, NA; Thompson memorandum to Wirth, May 10, 1941, File 0-32, Part IX, BBNP, RG 79, NA; NPS Press Release, July 18, 1941, File 0-32, Part IX, BBNP, RG 79, NA; Frank Quinn to Tillotson, December 18, File 0-32, Part IX, BBNP, RG 79, NA.

5. "Final Report of Big Bend Land Department," April 1, 1949, from files of Texas Parks and Wildlife Department, Austin, Texas (hereafter cited as TPWD).

began the serious work of land acquisition in September 1941.[6]

Unfortunately, the program was delayed by a court injunction before being jeopardized again by the United States entrance into World War II. Park supporters worried that patriotic Texans would demand that the Big Bend funds be diverted into the war effort. But these fears subsided somewhat when Amon Carter, chairman of the Big Bend Park Association, came out in favor of continuing the acquisition program. Carter's stand was important because he had delayed opening his organization's campaign because of the threat of war.[7]

The court injunction was brought about by J. H. King, state representative from Throckmorton and an opponent of the park. He sued State Comptroller George H. Sheppard to prevent him from paying out the $1,500,000 for park lands in Brewster County, arguing that the appropriation was unconstitutional. The Texas Court of Civil Appeals at Austin ruled against King in December 1941. Two months later the Texas Supreme Court refused to review the case and land acquisition at last could begin in earnest.[8]

The Texas State Parks Board and the Big Bend Land Department did not remain idle during the King litigation. Although the injunction had enjoined against land purchase, the Board had sent out option contracts to more than three thousand land owners.[9] Initial response to the mailings gave promise of a successful campaign. W. B. Hunter of San Angelo, Texas accepted the option price of one dollar and fifty cents per acre for his first thousand acres and do-

---

6. Fort Worth *Star-Telegram*, August 24, 1941. Frank Quinn was originally appointed to head the Big Bend Land Department but he resigned after a few weeks and from Austin coordinated the Texas State Parks Board activities in behalf of the land purchase program.

7. Fort Worth *Star-Telegram*, December 9, 1941.

8. Decision Number 9260, A. H. King, Appellant versus George H. Sheppard, Appellee, from District Court of Travis County, Texas, filed December 3, 1941 (transcript of decision in File 601, Part I, BBNP, RG 79, NA); Carter to Drury, February 23, 1942, File 601, Part I, BBNP, RG 79, NA; Frederick B. Isely to Donald E. Lee, March 9, 1942, File 601, Part I, BBNP, RG 79, NA; Lee to Isely, March 24, 1942, File 601, Part I, BBNP, RG 79, NA; Theodore Spector memorandum to Director, NPS, May 23, 1942, File 601, Part I, BBNP, RG 79, NA.

9. Quinn to Tillotson, December 18, 1941, File 0-32, Part IX, BBNP, RG 79, NA.

nated the remaining seventy-nine to the park. Thompson regarded Hunter's generosity as a "good omen."[10] When the King injunction was finally resolved in February 1942, the Board immediately purchased almost 300,000 acres, made offers for some 300,000 more, and initiated condemnation proceedings against an additional 45,000 acres.[11]

During the remaining six months the Big Bend Land Department obtained clear title to approximately two hundred sections of land per month. By the end of the year, only twenty-five sections remained unacquired.[12] Since some of the appropriated money had to be diverted to the Permanent School Fund as compensation for its mineral rights, the acreage for the Big Bend was adjusted from 788,682 to slightly less than 708,000.[13] By the end of 1942, the $1,500,000 appropriation was completely spent and Thompson and Townsend had done what many, including Park Service Director Newton B. Drury,[14] regarded as impossible. They had acquired ninety-eight per cent of the park lands in less than a year at an average cost of approximately two dollars per acre. Administrative costs had been approximately three and one-half per cent of the total, a record in efficient management for land purchase in a national

---

10. Quinn and Thompson to All Members of the Texas State Parks Board, December 15, 1941, File 0-32, Part IX, BBNP, RG 79, NA.

11. Carter to Drury, February 23, 1942, File 601, Part I, BBNP, RG 79, NA.

12. Thompson to D. M. Bennett, September 8, 1942, File 601, Part I, BBNP, RG 79, NA; "Final Report of Big Bend Land Department," April 1, 1949, from files of TPWD.

13. Quinn to Tillotson, August 18, 1941, File 0-32, Part IX, BBNP, RG 79, NA; Milton McColm memorandum to Director, NPS, September 2, 1941, File 601, Part I, BBNP, RG 79, NA; Quinn to Tillotson, December 18, 1941, File 0-32, Part IX, BBNP, RG 79, NA; Drury memorandum to Secretary of the Interior, December 22, 1942, File 601, 0-32, BBNP, RG 79, NA; Thompson to Tillotson, August 23, 1943, File 601, Part II, BBNP, RG 79, NA.

14. In a handwritten note at the bottom of a memorandum, Drury wrote, "I doubt if the money can be expended within a year." McColm memorandum to Director, NPS, September 2, 1941, File 601, Part I, BBNP, RG 79, NA. Actually, not all of the funds were spent at the end of twelve months. However, the few thousand dollars remaining was substantially less than that needed for outstanding options. As long as the Parks Board had the options, the funds could be used for purchasing park lands.

park.15

At the same time the Big Bend Land Department encountered some serious criticism. Several irate land owners wrote President Franklin D. Roosevelt during the land purchase program demanding the right to remain on their property. One woman, whose family had owned a ranch for forty years in Brewster County, asked: "How are we going to feed our sons and fellow men if they take our farms and ranches away from us? ... What good is parks? No rubber, no tourist to visit it and the country won't be any good if we don't win this war."[16] Another wrote:

> We have a modern home there [Brewster County] where our boys have lived all of their lives, they love it, and that cowboy [eldest son of the writer] in France needs to come back to the only home he has ever known when the war is won. If he can't go there, he will never feel as if he had come home. I wish that you might read some of his letters in which he writes about the hills, canyons, and trails that he longs for at home. The park project has passed since he entered the service, in fact his home was given away on D-Day when he was fighting for freedom and liberty.[17]

The mother concluded by asking the President if her family could remain on their ranch until the end of the war. "The park cannot be developed until the war is won so why should all of those honest, patriotic ranchmen have to move or give up their business of production while our boys are fighting?"[18]

Most of the transactions took place with a minimum of friction although several people discovered they had been victims of fraudulent land deals. A resident of Washington, D. C. found that her fifteen acres had been condemned for one dollar each, which she did not consider a fair price since she originally had paid a speculator

---

15. Tillotson memorandum to Director, NPS, August 31, 1942, File 601, Part I, BBNP, RG 79, NA; Tillotson memorandum to Director, NPS, November 10, 1942, File 601, Part I, BBNP, RG 79, NA.

16. Norah Walker to President of the United States of America, February 7, 1942, File 610, BBNP, RG 79, NA.

17. Mrs. W. T. Burnham to Roosevelt, March 5, 1945, File 601, Part III, BBNP, RG 79, NA.

18. *Ibid.* The Burnhams moved from the Big Bend area in 1945.

$225.00 for it.[19] E. E. Townsend informed an Ohio woman who asked to see her land that he could take her to it, but that she might have to lean up against it. Apparently she had purchased ten acres in the largely vertical Dead Horse Mountains. But a far more poignant story concerned three school teachers, each of whom had bought five acres in the Big Bend country for one hundred dollars per acre. They had intended to retire there only to discover too late that it too was on the top of a mountain peak and worth only a dollar per acre.[20]

Meanwhile, at the conclusion of the state's land acquisition program in September 1942, federal officials congratulated the Texas State Parks Board and the Big Bend Land Department for a job well done.[21] Drury stressed that the state should acquire the outstanding private holdings as soon as possible, pointing out that the key sections such as the several thousand acres at Castolon on the Rio Grande would seriously hinder the development of the park if left in private hands. The director further stated that this property should be purchased by the state before he could recommend the final establishment of Big Bend to the Secretary of the Interior.[22]

As it became apparent throughout the fall of 1942 and the winter of 1943 that the land purchase program had stagnated due to lack of money, Drury and Southwestern Regional Director M. R. Tillotson encouraged the State Parks Board to secure funds wherever possible. But Governor Coke Stevenson's administration had embarked on an economy drive and no further state appropriations seemed likely in the near future.[23] Efforts to have Amon Carter release the Big Bend

---

19. Lilla C. Singleton to Department of the Interior, March 5, 1943, File 610, BBNP, RG 79, NA.

20. Virginia Madison, *The Big Bend Country of Texas* (2nd ed.; New York: October House, 1968), p. 238.

21. Tillotson to Thompson, September 23, 1942, File 601, Part I, BBNP, RG 79, NA.

22. Drury memorandum to Regional Director, Region III, January 20, 1943, File 601, Part I, BBNP, RG 79, NA; Drury to Quinn, March 11, 1943, File 601, Part I, BBNP, RG 79, NA.

23. Tillotson memorandum to Director, NPS, February 6, 1943, File 601, Part I, BBNP, RG 79, NA; Drury memorandum to Regional Director, Region III, February 25, 1943, File 601, Part I, BBNP, RG 79, NA; Quinn to Drury, March 25, 1943, File 601, Part I, BBNP, RG 79, NA; Tillotson memorandum to Director, NPS, March 26, 1943, File 601, Part I, BBNP, RG 79, NA.

Park Association's Working Fund met a stubborn resistance from the chairman. Carter felt that he might need the money in the future and he rejected Drury's proposal that the Big Bend Park Association undertake another popular subscription campaign. "The public," he stated, "is too concerned with war causes, defense bond sales and similar patriotic movements to participate in any fund raising for parks."[24]

Other plans to raise money for the remaining Big Bend lands met a similar fate,[25] and on June 7, 1943 Drury reluctantly recommended to the Secretary of the Interior that the acres purchased so far be accepted, "with the understanding that the State Parks Board will continue to exert every effort to acquire the remaining privately owned lands within the project boundaries."[26] Drury had good reason to retain serious doubts about his recommendation. Regardless of the sincerity of the Parks Board, the agency could not force a "niggardly" legislature to grant the necessary funds any more than the Park Service could do the same with Congress. Nevertheless, the Secretary approved the proposal on June 24, 1943.[27]

As we have previously seen, much work remained to be done

---

24. Drury to Carter, March 20, 1943, File 601, Part I, BBNP, RG 79, NA; Carter to Drury, April 15, 1943, File 601, Part I, BBNP, RG 79, NA.

25. One money raising plan was a proposal by United States Representative Ewing Thomason to utilize $25,000 left over from a federal appropriation for the Texas Centennial. Another scheme called for a deficiency appropriation. See Lindsay C. Warren to Thomason, April 22, 1943, File 601, Part I, BBNP, RG 79, NA; Thompson, "Probable Funds to Complete Program," August 1, 1942, File 601, Part I, BBNP, RG 79, NA; "Excerpts from Minutes of the Meeting of the Texas State Parks Board, August 14, 1942, Austin, Texas," File 601, Part I, BBNP, RG 79, NA.

26. The Texas State Parks Board had promised Drury that it would strive to acquire all of the Big Bend acres. Quinn to Drury, March 25, 1943, File 601, Part I, BBNP, RG 79, NA; Drury memorandum to Secretary of the Interior, June 7, 1943, File 601, Part II, BBNP, RG 79, NA.

27. Drury to Quinn, April 1, 1943, File 601, Part I, BBNP, RG 79, NA; Drury to Wirth, October 14, 1943, File 610, BBNP, RG 79, NA; Tolson Departmental Memorandum, October 21, 1943, File 610, BBNP, RG 79, NA. Drury was anxious that Texas acquire all the land within the park. "If this is not done," he stated, "I am afraid the State will not feel obligated thereafter to acquire the remaining lands and it is apt to be a long time before the Federal Government will appropriate land acquisition funds for our use." Subsequent events proved Drury correct. Drury memorandum to Regional Director, Region III, January 20, 1943, File 601, Part I, BBNP, RG 79, NA.

before Big Bend could be established (i.e., the preparation of title insurance, checking title abstracts for accuracy, and the transfer of deeds and exclusive jurisdiction to the federal government).[28] By June 6, 1944 all work had been completed and the President and the Secretary of the Interior accepted the deed ceding jurisdiction to the United States. Six days later Big Bend National Park was officially established.

During the next five years the Texas State Parks Board acquired approximately one-half of the twenty-five sections desired. In the meantime, state officials had advised the Park Service that it would be unwise to approach the economy-minded legislature for another appropriation.[29] In 1947 State Senator H. L. Winfield, who had labored so effectively for the original $1,500,000 appropriation, supported a bill for an additional $125,000. He had refused to do so earlier because of a promise to the legislature that the $1,500,000 appropriation was all the state would have to pay for Big Bend.[30] However, the remaining private lands within the park had steadily risen from an estimated value of $75,000 in 1945 to almost $100,000 in two years.[31] But the 50th Legislature refused to appropriate more than $12,000. This, added to some $5,000 from other sources, enabled the Board to acquire another 7,680 acres by April 1, 1949. Almost 9,000 still remained in private hands, including the previously mentioned Castolon property and several other sections along the Rio Grande.[32]

---

28. Arthur Demaray to Thomason, July 7, 1943, File 501, BBNP, RG 79, NA.

29. H. L. Winfield to Quinn, April 2, 1945, File 601, Part III, BBNP, RG 79, NA.

30. Ross Maxwell memorandum to Regional Director, Region III, March 31, 1947, File 610, BBNP, RG 79, NA; Maxwell memorandum to Regional Director, Region III, April 22, 1947, File 610, BBNP, RG 79, NA.

31. Tillotson memorandum to Director, NPS, March 27, 1946, File 610, BBNP, RG 79, NA; Tillotson to James Record, June 11, 1947, File 610, BBNP, RG 79, NA.

32. Carter's organization had finally been persuaded to donate $3,000 and a couple thousand dollars equity was received for exchanges made for land outside the park. "Annual Report for Big Bend National Park, 1947," July 7, 1947, File 207, BBNP, RG 79, NA; Thompson to Maxwell, January 13, 1949, File 610, BBNP, RG 79, NA; "Final Report of Big Bend Land Department," April 1, 1949, from files of TPWD.

On April 13, 1949 Park Superintendent Ross A. Maxwell appeared before the Appropriations Committee of the Texas legislature to plead for $100,000 to purchase the above private holdings. He reminded the lawmakers of their obligation to the federal government and further pointed out that the Park Service faced a serious dilemma. It had spent $450,000 on improvements between 1948 and 1949—mostly essential roads which inadvertently had caused private lands to increase in value. Whereas the owners of the Castolon tract had been willing to accept $39,006 for their land in 1942, they now wanted $125,000.[33] These and other key holdings seriously jeopardized the development of the park's $10,600,000 master plan. They also blocked visitor access to leading scenic features of the park, including the mouth of Boquillas Canyon.[34] Nevertheless, Maxwell failed to influence a legislature content to let the federal government assume responsibility for land purchases.

Throughout the latter 1940s Congress had appropriated money for the purchase of lands at the northern entrance to the park at Persimmon Gap, but these funds were restricted to road construction and right-of-ways.[35] The troublesome Castolon property therefore was left untouched. These 3,756 acres were located on the international boundary and were consequently a constant source of trouble. Hundreds of Mexican laborers made illegal crossings here to work on adjacent ranches and farms. Some processed wax from candelilla plants and rubber from guayule plants and smuggled their products out of the park into Texas and Mexico.[36]

Cattle and sheep grazing and the manufacturing of wax and rubber soon depleted the sparse natural vegetation of the private lands. The longer they remained outside of federal control, the worse the situation became. For example, if private owners decided to make improvements on their land, they doubtless would demand exorbi-

---

33. The assessed value of the Castolon property in 1949 was only $60,000, however.

34. Maxwell, "Remarks to be Given before the Appropriations Committee, State Legislature—in Support of a Bill to Appropriate $100,000 with which to Purchase the Remaining Private Lands in Big Bend National Park," April 13, 1949, Big Bend National Park Library (hereafter cited as BBNP Lib).

35. U. S., *Statutes at Large*, LXIII, pp. 679-680.

36. Lemuel A. Garrison memorandum to Regional Director, Region III, January 29, 1954, BBNP Lib.

tant compensation. Moreover, the Park Service became especially alarmed over the discovery that one individual planned to construct a hunting lodge. Also, land valued at $55,000 in 1942 had risen to $257,000 over the next twelve years.[37]

Obviously, something had to be done before these private holdings further increased in value. By August 1953, Congress realized that the state had no intention of acquiring the much needed property. It authorized the Secretary of the Interior "to procure, in such manner as he may consider to be in the public interest, the remaining non-federal land." Accordingly, by 1972 the Park Service had purchased, condemned, and accepted donation of the remaining acres. All told, the federal government had acquired 8,561.75 acres at a total cost of $300,375. These lands constituted only one per cent of the park acreage, yet required sixteen per cent of the approximately $1,822,120 expended for the Big Bend lands. The average cost per acre of the federal acquisitions had indeed been expensive—slightly over $35.00.[38] After a land acquisition program which lasted nearly four decades, Big Bend National Park at last belonged exclusively to the public.[39]

---

37. *Ibid.*; "Final Report of Big Bend Land Department," April 1, 1949, from files of TPWD.

38. U. S., *Statutes at Large*, LXVII, p. 497; Joe Brown, NPS to the author, January 10, 1974.

39. There are, however, private mineral interests still within the park boundaries. But they concern only about one-half of one per cent of the park acreage. And furthermore, the Secretary of the Interior has to authorize mineral exploitation in the national parks, which is not likely. Joe Brown, NPS, to the author, December 13, 1973. In 1972 the last land was acquired through condemnation. J. F. Carithers, NPS, to the author, December 6, 1973.

IV The Publicity Campaign

Only recently historians have realized what archaeologists, geographers, and anthropologists have known for some time—the environment is a valuable document whose study tells much about the human experience. Whether communities have altered, destroyed, or simply left the environment alone reveals to the careful observer their values and priorities. These are especially reflected in the arguments for and against national parks. An examination of the supporters and opponents of Big Bend National Park during the publicity campaign from 1936 to 1945 provides an in-depth look at environmental attitudes at the national, state, and local levels.[1]

Press releases and other news stories on the proposed Big Bend Park concentrated on its biological, geological, international, scenic, and other unique features. The Chisos mountains and surrounding plains, for instance, received wide coverage since they formed the only "biological island" in the national park system. The island contained species of animals, birds, and plants which existed nowhere else in the United States, or, in some cases, the world. Two examples were the Colima Warbler, whose northern range in the western hemisphere extends only as far as the Chisos, and the weeping juniper, which also grows in Brazil. Geologically, the Big Bend country provides a natural classroom of earth history which is fascinating to amateur and professional alike. The only geological characteristic not represented is glaciation. Numerous newspaper articles and

---

1. Roderick Nash has written a good synthesis of American attitudes toward wilderness. See his *Wilderness and the American Mind* (rev. ed.; New Haven: Yale University Press, 1982). He also perceptively deals with environmental attitudes in "The State of Environmental History," Herbert J. Bass, ed., *The State of American History* (Chicago: Quadrangle Books, 1970).

photographs depicted the fossil remains of dinosaur skeletons and giant oyster shells, the latter measuring over twelve square feet. The international appeal of Big Bend received considerable news space outside of Texas, especially during World War II, when the idea of a "peace" park symbolized to many Americans the allied cause against the forces of tyranny. Moreover, the creation of an international park with Mexico would complement the Waterton-Glacier Park established in 1932 on the Canadian border.[2]

Texans took considerable pride in the scenic attractions of the Big Bend. Horace Morelock, president of Sul Ross College at Alpine, considered the view from the park's south rim "the most beautiful panorama on the American continent." A favorite source of comparison was Big Bend's Santa Elena Canyon, which several Texas newspapers condescendingly rated equal to the Grand Canyon of Arizona. Some Texans maintained that Big Bend's beauty not only surpassed that of the Grand Canyon, but other outstanding scenic areas as well. When Coke Stevenson, then a member of the Texas House of Representatives, made a plea in 1937 for the passage of his appropriation bill, he emphasized the money would help establish a park that would "excel Yellowstone." E. O. Thompson, a member of the state railroad commission, proclaimed the Texas Big Bend an area "that Europe, even with its Alps, cannot match." An editorial in the Woodville, Texas *Booster* asked, "Why go to Europe anytime?" The paper regarded the Big Bend as "far ahead of either Europe or Asia in beauty and sublimity."[3]

---

2. Austin *American*, May 1, 1936; Alpine *Avalanche*, May 14, 1936; Fort Worth *Star-Telegram*, December 6, 1937; December 2, 1938; Dallas *Morning News*, October 31, 1937; Galveston *Tribune*, September 11, 1937; Leo McClatchy, "Interesting Things About Big Bend" (ms), June 5, 1936, File 501-04, Big Bend National Park, Record Group 79, National Archives Building (hereafter cited as BBNP, RG 79, NA); NPS Press Release, April 26, 1936, File 0-32, Part III, BBNP, RG 79, NA; Denver *Post*, March 7, 1937; San Antonio *Express*, February 28, 1937; March 7, 1937; Dallas *Morning News*, February 28, 1937; Fort Worth *Star-Telegram*, February 28, 1937; New York *Times*, November 24, 1935; Butte, Montana *Daily Post*, March 14, 1936; Miami, Florida *News*, September 27, 1942; *Christian Science Monitor*, July 21, 1944; San Francisco *Call Bulletin*, June 20, 1944.

3. Fort Worth *Star-Telegram*, September 10, 1937. Morelock gave credit for the statement to Herbert Maier of the NPS. See "Big Bend National Park Bulletin of Information," September 10, 1937, File 0-32, Part V, BBNP, RG 79, NA. Santa Elena is often referred to as the "Grand Canyon of the Rio Grande."

Some Park Service officials reacted in a similar manner to Big Bend's scenery and other attractions. One Park Service publicist wrote a syndicated article that appeared in over two hundred Texas newspapers. He declared that "The Big Bend section is noted for scenic grandeur. Nowhere in America are more picturesque peaks, gorges, and valleys." Geologist Carroll Wegemann said that the region was one of the "few areas in the United States" which remained "unchanged by the advance of modern civilization." Roger Toll, superintendent of Yellowstone and chief investigator of prospective park sites, wrote that the Big Bend was "unspoiled." Minor R. Tillotson, regional director of the Park Service in the Southwest, regularly referred to the new park as the "last frontier of America."[4]

These comments by the Park Service, the Texas press, and other individuals contained much exaggeration, if not outright fantasy. Ross Maxwell, the first superintendent of Big Bend from 1944 to 1952, acknowledged that the park "can't boast of awe-inspiring beauty which is found in some of the national parks, but it has scientific phenomena and scenic beauty mingled with historic incidents along the Texas-Mexico frontier that give it a charm and color that is not known in any other park." Maxwell remarked that he personally knew of several canyons in the United States which had "greater splendor" than Santa Elena. Concerning the unspoiled nature of the country, even today some of the land remains grassless as a consequence of overgrazing and bears the descriptive label "desert pavement." The statement about Big Bend as America's last frontier had a tremendous romantic appeal, but like some of the other observations, it was inaccurate. Alaska, for instance, more fully deserves

---

Palestine *Herald Press*, April 17, 1938; Austin *American*, April 14, 1936; San Antonio *News*, November 3, 1937; San Angelo *Standard-Times*, March 3, 1939; Colorado City *Record*, April 28, 1939; Amarillo *News*, April 15, 1939; Corpus Christi *Caller*, April 15, 1939; Fort Worth *Star-Telegram*, September 19, 1937; Shamrock *Texan*, April 15, 1939; Alpine *Avalanche*, March 5, 1937; Fort Worth *Star-Telegram*, July 28, 1937; Woodville *Booster*, June 1, 1939.

4. Leo A. McClatchy, "Interesting Things About the Big Bend" (ms), File 501-04, BBNP, RG 79, NA; NPS Press Release, April 26, 1936, File 0-32, Part III, BBNP, RG 79, NA; Fort Worth *Star-Telegram*, April 26, 1936; Dallas *Morning News*, April 26, 1936; Erle Kauffman, "The Big Bend of the Rio," *American Forests* (advance proof), File 0-32, Part I, BBNP, RG 79, NA; Fort Worth *Star-Telegram*, September 29, 1940; Alpine *Avalanche*, May 8, 1942.

that designation.[5]

Although the Big Bend publicity organizers tried to eliminate the unpleasant or controversial, occasionally an adverse item slipped through. In 1937 newspapers reported that a black bear had stampeded nineteen goats off a 3,000 foot precipice in the park. The "goat tragedy" came at an inopportune time, for the NPS had just convinced the Texas Fish and Wildlife Department to place the black bear on the protected game animal list. The Park Service regretted that the story had been given to the press since it "will not be appreciated by local ranchmen."[6]

The effort to emphasize only the positive features sometimes resulted in distortion of reality. In 1935 the Park Service commissioned a movie of Big Bend. But instead of instructing the film makers to emphasize its desert qualities, which comprise the greater part of the area, one official requested that most of the footage shot should deal with "the very interesting forest color" in the Chisos Mountains. Apparently he felt tourists would not respond to an arid vacation land. Yet when foggy weather interrupted the work of a *Life* magazine crew doing a photographic essay on Big Bend, one NPS critic objected to a newspaper story on this because it clashed with the image publicists had created that Big Bend was a year-round park with continuous sunshine.[7]

As much as the Park Service hierarchy tried to quell it, unfavorable publicity continued to hamper the Big Bend park movement. In December 1937 Senator Morris Sheppard received word that there were fresh gold and cinnabar strikes in the Big Bend. Although the news was baseless, it nevertheless caused a real estate boom in the area and convinced some that the region was far from submarginal

---

5. Virginia Madison, *The Big Bend Country of Texas* (2nd ed.; New York: October House, 1968), p. 240; Maxwell memorandum to Regional Director, Region III, October 5, 1944, File 501–02, BBNP, RG 79, NA; Jack Hope, "Big Bend: A Nice Place to Visit," *Audubon*, LXXV (July, 1973), pp. 38–39.

6. NPS Press Release, September 2, 1937, File 0–32, Part V, BBNP, RG 79, NA; W. B. McDougall memorandum to Victor Cahalane, January 9, 1940, File 0–32, Part VIII, BBNP, RG 79, NA; Hillory Tolson to Maier, November 12, 1937, File 0–32, Part V, BBNP, RG 79, NA.

7. Maier to E. E. Townsend, April 20, 1936, File 0–32, Part III, BBNP, RG 79, NA; Dallas *Morning News*, January 17, 1945; Tillotson memorandum to Director, NPS, January 22, 1945, File 501–03, Part III, BBNP, RG 79, NA.

as the NPS claimed. The state land commissioner later added to the difficulties of land purchase by permitting mineral speculators to file on the park acres.[8]

The outbreak of World War II found even the crusading journalist Drew Pearson alligned against the Big Bend. In his column, "The Washington Merry-Go-Round," Pearson wrote an article titled, "Gas Masks or Parks?" Wartime severely tests the sanctity of the national parks as the military demands access to as many of the country's resources as possible. In the Big Bend area a wax taken from the candelilla plant was used as a sealing compound in gas masks. According to the columnist, a patriotic New York millionaire had set up a factory to exploit the weed, only to be told by the NPS that he had violated Service policy which forbids the destruction of a park's natural resources. Pearson dramatically concluded, "So now the deer and the antelope, instead of gas mask wearers, will have the benefit of the candelilla."[9]

As it turned out, Pearson had not received all of the facts, for much more candelilla was available in sections of Brewster and Presidio Counties outside of the park boundaries. Also, the so-called millionaire conducted a rather unstable enterprise and failed to pay for some of his machinery and other processing equipment.[10] But the Big Bend weathered these and other challenges due partly to the attraction Americans have for their national parks and also to the well organized publicity activities at the national, regional, and local level.

Isabelle F. Story, Information Officer for the NPS, and her staff did a thorough job of keeping Big Bend before the public.[11] Articles

---

8. Sheppard to Arno B. Cammerer, December 17, 1937, File 0-32, Part V, BBNP, RG 79, NA; Arthur Demaray to Sheppard, December 31, 1937, File 0-32, Part V, BBNP, RG 79, NA; Houston *Press*, August 13, 1938; El Paso *Herald-Post*, August 18, 1938; Fort Worth *Star-Telegram*, August 21, 1938.

9. Dallas *Morning News*, October 26, 1942.

10. Eugene Thompson to J. V. Ash, November 1, 1942, File 501, BBNP, RG 79, NA.

11. The Park Service provided a series of twenty-eight Sunday features on the established national parks complete with pictures "in the hope the civic pride of Texans will be sufficiently aroused to put over the Big Bend park." Photographs of Big Bend as well as copy on the park were made available. See Story to Carl P. Russell, March 7, 1938, File 0-32, Part V, BBNP, RG 79, NA; Conrad Wirth to Regional Officer, Region III, August 7, 1937, File 0-32, Part

and editorials on the park appeared in newspapers from coast to coast with several excellent pictorial features on the scenic attractions of the Big Bend area. One editorial carried by several dailies raised the following question: "Why should anyone ever leave Florida (or California)?" The answer—"They both go to see Big Bend."[12]

Other publicity activities of the Park Service included the construction of a scale model relief map which was displayed at the Texas Centennial Exposition in Dallas and later in Austin in the state capitol's rotunda during the 1939 legislative session when major park legislation was being considered. According to some observers, the authentic model had a favorable influence on the legislators's actions. The Texas Gulf Sulphur Company contributed $4,500 to pay for the production of a color film on Big Bend. The film project was the first the Park Service had undertaken in several years. Other movies taken by individuals and organizations interested in Big Bend were also shown throughout the state. The visual presentations, accompanied by informed and entertaining lecturers from the NPS and booster groups, did much to create interest in Big Bend National Park.[13]

One of the most effective publicity techniques was the utilization of well known personalities to promote the Big Bend. The noted Southwestern writer J. Frank Dobie accompanied the *National Ge-*

IV, BBNP, RG 79, NA.

12. The following are only a sample of the non-Texas newspaper coverage for Big Bend—New York *Times*, November 24, 1935; *Christian Science Monitor*, January 30, 1936; July 21, 1944; Butte, Montana *Daily Post*, March 14, 1936; Denver *Post*, January 31, 1936; March 7, 1937; September 27, 1942; Philadelphia *Evening Public Ledger*, January 10, 1938; Miami, Florida *News*, September 27, 1941; Oakland, California *Tribune*, July 28, 1944; New York *Herald Tribune*, September 12, 1944; Detroit *News*, January 21, 1945; Cumberland, Maryland *Times*, November 13, 1944; Charleston, West Virginia *Gazette*, November 12, 1944; Mankato, Minnesota *Free Press*, November 11, 1944; Alexandria, Louisiana *Town Talk*, November 9, 1944; Portsmouth, Virginia *Star*, November 11, 1944.

13. Earl Trager memorandum to Russell, May 9, 1936, File 0-32, Part III, BBNP, RG 79, NA; H. L. Winfield to W. F. Ayres, March 13, 1939, File 0-32, Part VI, BBNP, RG 79, NA; Tom L. Beauchamp to Ayres, March 14, 1939, File 0-32, Part VI, BBNP, RG 79, NA; Cammerer memorandum to E. K. Burlew, November 12, 1935, File 0-32, Part II, BBNP, RG 79, NA; San Angelo *Standard Times*, April 12, 1938; Alpine *Avalanche*, April 15, 1938; March 2, 1939; Fort Worth *Star-Telegram*, June 4, 1938; March 30, 1939; Fort Stockton *Pioneer*, April 7, 1939; Eden *Echo*, May 25, 1939; Wichita Falls *Times*, June 4, 1939.

ographic party which investigated the region in 1938. Dobie also spent the winter of 1939 in the Big Bend country working on a book on longhorn cattle. Robert T. Hill, the prominent geologist-explorer who wrote the *Century* magazine article that helped arouse interest in the idea of a Big Bend park, offered to publicize the area in a weekly newspaper column. The University of California's Herbert E. Bolton, a foremost historian of the Borderlands and the American West, toured the Big Bend region while retracing Coronado's journey through the Trans-Pecos country. But the major coup for the NPS was the appointment of Walter Prescott Webb as a historical consultant on the Big Bend. Webb was a professor of history at the University of Texas and ranked alongside of Bolton and Frederick Jackson Turner as an authority on the American West.[14]

Webb accepted the new post at twenty dollars per day for a two month assignment while on leave of absence for the 1936–1937 academic year. The Park Service wanted Webb to write a narrative history of the Trans-Pecos area from Spanish exploration to the present emphasizing the Big Bend country and its peculiar effect on people.[15] He eagerly plunged into the task and by the middle of April had written two articles which were released on consecutive Sundays in newspapers from coast to coast. In typical fashion, Webb did not let facts stand in the way of literary expression. Fortunately, or otherwise, Service geologists corrected his "vivid imagination" whenever it clashed with geological fact.[16] Despite these censures,

---

14. Maxwell to Director, NPS, attention of Trager, March 7, 1938, File 0–32, Part V, BBNP, RG 79, NA; Balmorhea *Texan*, February 24, 1939; Trager memorandum to Regional Director, Region III, January 16, 1939, File 0–32, Part VI, BBNP, RG 79, NA; Tillotson to Bolton, June 6, 1944, File 204, BBNP, RG 79, NA; Herbert Kahler to Newton B. Drury, June 23, 1944, File 204, BBNP, RG 79, NA; Kahler to Bolton, June 23, 1944, File 204, BBNP, RG 79, NA.

15. Maier to Webb, April 26, 1937, Box 2M260, Webb Papers, Barker Texas History Collection, University of Texas, Austin (hereafter cited as Webb Papers, Barker Collection).

16. An unidentified reader of Webb's first article wrote, "Webb shows a vivid imagination with little regard for the facts." The reader noted that "It was not a 'blast' [interior quotes are from Webb's unedited draft] that wrecked the mountain. 'Explosive gas' did not explode. There was no 'supernatural fury.' Waters did not go down 'to the internal heat to return as steam bringing up molten lava.'" The critic concluded, "All this may be 'fine writing' but his geology is all haywire." Anonymous Critique of Webb's "The Big Bend" (no date), Box 2M260, Webb Papers, Barker Collection.

Webb's style prevailed and the first article, which appeared on April 18, 1937, is the best of the three he wrote for the NPS, and demonstrates the wide range of Webb's intellectual and literary abilities, even though he did rankle a few scientists.[17]

The second article, released on April 25, is largely concerned with various passages made through the canyons of the Rio Grande, particularly Santa Elena. Even before beginning work as a consulting historian, the idea of personally making a float trip through Santa Elena had intrigued Webb.[18] He asked Everett Ewing Townsend to research previous canyon expeditions. Townsend found that before the Civil War a Swede descended the Rio Grande from El Paso to Brownsville to avoid hostile Apaches. Over the years others followed including Texas Rangers, geologists, and army and Border Patrol personnel. Most reported uneventful passages but several had drowned in the confines of Santa Elena Canyon, noted for its massive 250 foot rock slide and fierce undertow.[19]

In April 1937 Webb employed Thomas Skaggs of McCamey, Texas to organize and guide an expedition through Santa Elena Canyon.[20] Skaggs was an experienced riverman who had successfully made the canyon passage several times. The Park Service endorsed the project because it would help round out Webb's knowledge of the area and also would focus national publicity on the Big Bend park movement. An additional factor in its favor was that Webb himself

---

17. Webb originally had written one long article but its length necessitated dividing it into two parts. Leo McClatchy to Webb, (no date), File 4, Webb Papers, Texas State Archives, Austin; Webb, "The Big Bend of Texas," NPS Press Release, April 18, 1937, File 501, BBNP, RG 79, NA.

18. Webb, "The Big Bend of Texas," NPS Press Release, April 25, 1937, File 501, BBNP, RG 79, NA.

19. Thomas Skaggs to E. E. Townsend, March 30, 1937, File 2, Webb Papers, TSA. Larry McMurtry accurately refers to Webb as a "symbolic frontiersman." This is manifested in his desire "to do at least one foolish thing each year." The river trip is very much a part of this quest for the nineteenth century frontier. See McMurtry, *In a Narrow Grave: Essay on Texas* (New York: Simon and Schuster, 1968), p. 43.

20. Townsend, "Data on Passages Made Through the Canyons of the Rio Grande," August 1936, File 2, Webb Papers, TSA. Webb obtained other reports as well. See H. W. Johnson and Henry M. Zellar memorandum to Commanding Officer, Fort D. A. Russell, Texas, April 28, 1930 on the subject "Reconnaisance of Grand Canyon of Santa Helena," and Nick D. Collaer to District Director, U. S. Immigration Service, El Paso, July 30, 1930, File 2, Webb Papers, TSA.

financed the expedition.[21]

Members of the Webb party received advice from many different quarters about the dangers to be encountered. An old cowboy, Uncle Jimmie Shipman, warned that the rampaging water "goes this way against one side of the cliff and plunges back against the other side, and I'm telling you, boys, YOU KAINT MAKE IT." Joe Lane, the cook and also an experienced riverman, was kidded that the river was so dangerous that he was certain to suffer death by drowning. Then, whenever a catfish was caught, it would be a part of old Joe. The local undertaker, upon hearing of the proposed trip, supposedly went out and bought a new suit.[22]

But Skaggs assured Webb that the trip was safer than driving on the highway. The construction of dams along the upper portions and tributaries had taken much of the ferocity out of the river. The possibility of flash flooding still existed but the approaching waters echoed a warning against the canyon walls giving one plenty of time to reach safety.[23] In fact, Skaggs even needled Webb "to pour on the publicity about the dangers of the canyon," that "turbulent, terrorizing, tragedy-marked Canyon of the Santa Helena."[24] Skaggs was of the opinion that the passage would be "rather tame but picturesque." He volunteered along with Joe Lane to "run any rapids, capsize our boats, or perform any stunts" in order to provide exciting film footage for the movie man that was to accompany the

---

21. Maier to Director, NPS, April 24, 1937; Wirth to Regional Officer, Region III, April 27, 1937; NPS Press Release, May 7, 1937, File 0-32, Part IV, BBNP, RG 79, NA.

22. Joe Lane further reported that "half the people he talks to about the trip offer him sympathy and are afraid he will not come back; the other half hopes he gets drowned and are afraid he will come back." Skaggs to Webb, May 11, 1937, File 2, Webb Papers, TSA; Skaggs to Webb, April 11, 1937; May 10, 1937, File 1, Webb Papers, TSA. In addition to Skaggs and Lane, Webb was accompanied by James W. Metcalf, Acting Chief Inspector of the U. S. Immigration Service Border Patrol. Metcalf was a last minute replacement for William R. Hogan of the NPS who was detained on agency business elsewhere and could not make the trip. Webb, "Materials Prepared as a Basis for a Guide to Points of Interest in the Proposed BBNP," File 2, Webb Papers, TSA.

23. Skaggs to Webb, April 3, 1937, File 1, Webb Papers, TSA; Skaggs to Webb, May 11, 1937; Webb, "Materials Prepared as a Basis for a Guide to Points of Interest in the Proposed BBNP," File 2, Webb Papers, TSA.

24. Skaggs to Webb, May 11, 1937, File 2, Webb Papers, TSA.

expedition.[25]

Despite these assurances, Webb made extensive preparations for any dangers that might arise. He purchased two specially constructed steel, flat-bottomed boats with air chambers and named them the *Big Bend* and *Cinco de Mayo*. The boats were sixteen and thirteen feet long, respectively, and could be dismantled into sections for portaging over the rock slide inside the canyon. The four men were to wear life preservers, while a speedboat waited at the mouth of the canyon in case of an emergency. A Coast Guard plane would check on their progress and would watch for rising water and other hazards. A communication system was devised to enable the party to signal the plane above with red and white flags.[26] Since smugglers and bandits were also prevalent, a .45 Colt would be taken "for general use and signaling if necessary."[27]

Mrs. Walter Prescott Webb still had misgivings about the whole affair. Skaggs wrote her husband to alleviate these fears. "I note what Mrs. Webb says about the trip, and that the *Titanic* also had air chambers. Yes, but we have no icebergs on the Rio Grande in May." As long as the expedition took the time to portage over the rock slide, Skaggs continued, there was "absolutely no danger."[28] Perhaps these words calmed Webb's wife on Sunday morning, May 15 as her husband embarked down the Rio Grande. But her peace of mind was short-lived.

News of the expedition's progress had not reached the outside by Monday evening because of a breakdown in communication and the press assumed the worst. One headline read: "No Word from Four Explorers: Boatmen still Unreported after Rowing into Danger Zone of the Rio Grande." Another stated: "Four Scientists Missing on Dangerous River Trip." Actually, the men were never in real danger other than the hazards of navigating the bulky vessels down the swift river, portaging over the rockslide, or being struck

---

25. Their antics were not necessary, however, as the Paramount man did not make the trip. Only still photographs were taken. Skaggs to Webb, May 9, 1937, File 1, Webb Paper, TSA.

26. NPS Press Release, May 7, 1937, File 0–32, Part IV, BBNP, RG 79, NA; Austin *Dispatch*, May 16, 1937.

27. Skaggs to Webb, April 29, 1937, File 1, Webb Papers, TSA.

28. Skaggs to Webb, May 2, 1937, File 1, Webb Papers, TSA.

by boulders plummeting "like comets" from the 2,000 foot canyon walls. They successfully completed the journey by Tuesday noon and Webb emerged from the experience an even more enthusiastic supporter of the park than previously. He described the desolate region as having "a peculiar romantic quality" and added that the most beautiful country he had ever seen was in the depths of Santa Elena Canyon.[29]

The publicity efforts of several prominent political figures likewise aided the Big Bend movement. When the British king and queen visited Washington in 1939, Texas's eccentric governor, W. Lee "Pappy" O'Daniel, sent a telegram to "King George, care of the White House" and invited him to come visit Texas and the Big Bend. O'Daniel also encouraged the King to "bring the Queen along." The Governor further publicized the park in 1939 in connection with the signing of legislation making it possible to transfer the Big Bend lands in fee simple title to the federal government. He used four giant pens forty-two inches long, one of which was later presented to President Roosevelt.[30]

The President gave an additional boost to the park in 1939 when he wrote to the Texas legislature, via O'Daniel, encouraging its members to take positive action on measures essential to Big Bend. Also, from time to time the President discussed the park with Texas congressmen and senators, always maintaining an optimistic attitude regarding the eventual success of the movement. Of major importance to Roosevelt was the international aspect, which coincided with the "Good Neighbor" foreign policy for the western

---

29. Fort Worth *Star-Telegram*, May 18, 1937; Oklahoma City *Times*, May 18, 1937; El Paso *Times*, May 17, 1937; Oklahoma City *Oklahoman*, May 19, 1937; Houston *Post*, February 20, 1938. Webb's hometown paper carried the headline "Webb Defying Canyon Perils," Austin *Statesman*, May 17, 1937. Much more indicative of the "perils" faced by the "scientists" and "explorers" is the following passage from Webb: "A bottle of champagne had been brought, with which to christen the boats when they were put into the water, but after some discussion, it was decided that it would be a shame to waste the champagne and so it was used to toast the success of the venture." Webb, "Materials Prepared as a Basis for a Guide to Points of Interest in the Proposed BBNP," File 2, Webb Papers TSA.

30. Austin *State Observer*, June 12, 1939; Harlingen *Valley Morning Star*, May 13, 1939; Galveston *News*, May 13, 1939; Fort Worth *Star-Telegram*, May 14, 1939; O'Daniel to Roosevelt, October 17, 1940, File 0-32, Part VIII, BBNP, RG 79, NA.

Another prominent, national supporter of Big Bend was Secretary of the Interior Harold Ickes. He came to Texas in the fall of 1937 to dedicate a New Deal water reservoir project, but much of his speech concerned Big Bend National Park. Besides mentioning the unique, scenic, and international possibilities of the area, he chided Texans for doing nothing about it. The Secretary said that even if Texas had to pay five times the estimated value of the park lands (then $1,000,000), he believed that it would still be an excellent investment since the federal government would develop and maintain it without further expense to the state. Tourists would subsequently flock to the Big Bend. "Give me the profits that would accrue to the citizens of Texas from the establishment of this park," Ickes said, "and I would undertake to buy the land necessary and turn it over to the Federal Government even if I had to raise ten million dollars for it." The Secretary continued: "Conservative investors would fight each other for an opportunity to put their money into a proposition that would pay so richly and inevitably."[32]

The economic argument for a national park was the one heard most often. Early in the Big Bend park movement Arno B. Cammerer, Director of the Park Service, spoke before a partisan gathering in El Paso of representatives from Texas chambers of commerce and city and county officials. He told of severe economic conditions in Utah during the early twentieth century which forced the Mormons to sell eggs for five cents a dozen and to use surplus butter as wagon axle grease. Prosperity returned soon after 1919 when Zion National Park was established and provided a market for the area's products. Another NPS official calculated that park visitors to Big Bend would spend at least $2,388,000 annually in the state, a figure which would justify a capital investment of $79,600,000 on the basis of a three per cent return. Yet all Texans would have to pay was from one to one and one-half million dollars.[33]

Texas newspapers likewise pushed the economic argument. The

---

32. Speech delivered by Secretary of the Interior Ickes at the dedication of the Buchanan and Inks Dams, October 16, 1937, Records of the Office of the Secretary of the Interior, 12–29, National Parks, Big Bend, Texas, General, Part II, RG 48, NA.

33. El Paso *Herald-Post*, November 10, 1936; Tillotson, "The Big Bend National Park as an Asset to the State of Texas" (ms), March 27, 1941, File 0–32, Part VIII, BBNP, RG 79, NA.

Fort Worth *Star-Telegram* reported that in Wyoming one-third of the out-of-state tourist income came from visitors to Yellowstone and Grand Teton alone. The same paper ran a series of articles on the importance of tourist travel to Texas and noted that Big Bend "likely offers more surprises to the visitor than any other attraction in or out of Texas." The San Antonio *Express* found that in 1936 tourism was the second largest industry in the state and that it grossed $446,000,000. At the same time, crude oil produced revenues of $450,000,000 and agricultural crops $284,000,000. The *Express* saw no reason Big Bend could not generate $4,000,000 during its first year and possibly boost tourism into a tie with crude oil as the state's leading business.[34]

The Texas press especially supported political measures on Big Bend's behalf. For example, in 1937 editorials overwhelmingly supported the first appropriation bill for $750,000.[35] The 45th Legislature passed it, but Governor James V. Allred vetoed the legislation. Following the Governor's action, a few newspapers supported his decision. None opposed a national park as such, but rather the means of financing it. They agreed with Allred that there simply was not enough money in the state treasury.[36] But the majority of the dailies strongly criticized the Governor's decision. The El Paso *Times* and the San Antonio *Express* recounted the economic reasons why Big Bend was a good investment. "Governor Allred says we can't afford it," the *Times* concluded. "Did you ever hear of such smallness of

---

34. The following are only a small sample of the newspapers that emphasized economic arguments for Big Bend: El Paso *Herald-Post*, November 10, 1936; Galveston *Tribune*, December 12, 1936; Houston *Post*, May 28, 1937; Houston *Press*, October 21, 1937; San Angelo *Times*, February 23, 1938; San Antonio *Evening News*, November 16, 1938; Del Rio *Evening News*, December 12, 1938; Abilene *Reporter-News*, December 1, 1938; Dallas *Times-Herald*, December 1, 1938; San Antonio *Express*, September 12, 1938; Dallas *Morning News*, March 3, 1939; Colorado City *Record*, April 28, 1939; Dallas *Dispatch Journal*, May 18, 1939; Graham *Reporter*, June 24, 1939; Fort Worth *Star-Telegram*, July 31, 1938; January 26, 1937; San Antonio *Express*, March 24, 1937; February 25, 1939.

35. Representative editorials favoring the $750,000 appropriation can be found in the Fort Worth *Star-Telegram*, February 20, 1937; San Antonio *Express*, February 23, 1937; April 12, 1937; June 6, 1937; Houston *Post*, February 22, 1937; April 12, 1937; May 28, 1937; Tyler *Morning Telegraph*, April 13, 1937; Alpine *Avalanche*, December 4, 1936; El Paso *Herald-Post*, May 28, 1937.

36. Dallas *Times-Herald*, June 9, 1937; Brownwood *Bulletin*, June 11, 1937.

vision in a governor's office?"[37]

During the nine years between Big Bend's authorization in 1935 and final establishment in 1944, Texas newspapers gave extensive publicity to further legislative proposals and fund raising projects. In addition, the press featured articles and photographs on what there was to see and do in the Big Bend.[38] An editorial in the Lufkin *Daily News* summed up the attitude most Texans had for their proposed park: "It is a far cry from the piney woods of East Texas to the rugged grandeur of the Big Bend country, but the development of splendid possibilities out there for a national park of ultimate worldwide fame is an undertaking meriting the support of all sections of Texas."[39]

Individuals interested in Big Bend, but not necessarily members of organized groups, did much to publicize the park. J. Edgar Kimsey, postmaster at Texon and known also as cowboy artist "Las Vegas Kim," drew western sketches for anyone who contributed one dollar to the popular subscription campaign. One of the recipients of a drawing was Governor Allred. Roy and W. E. Swift from South Texas swam a treacherous twenty-one mile stretch of the Rio Grande through Santa Elena Canyon. They waded, used innertubes for some portions of their trip, and roped themselves over impassable spots. A minister from Marfa, Texas, the Reverend Milton Hill, and his wife and friends made three separate float trips through the major canyons in the park. Hill found that Mariscal Canyon "has more variety and rock sculpture" than Santa Elena. A Boston author, Rollo Walter Brown, wrote a book entitled *I Travel by Train* and devoted several pages to Big Bend and Sul Ross College where he had taught one summer session. Brown discovered that the natural beauty of West Texas girls surpassed all other regions of the United States. He

---

37. San Antonio *Express*, June 10, 1937; El Paso *Times*, June 9, 1937.

38. Dallas *Morning News*, October 31, 1937; September 25, 1938; October 1, 1940; Austin *Statesman*, April 7, 1939; Houston *Press*, April 17, 1939; Wichita Falls *Record News*, May 22, 1939; Amarillo *Daily News*, November 25, 1938; El Paso *Times*, October 17, 1937; Dallas *Morning News*, July 6, 1944; July 7, 1944; July 9, 1944; July 10, 1944; October 30, 1938; April 24, 1938; Houston *Chronicle*, November 28, 1937; Galveston *Tribune*, September 11, 1937; Austin *American*; May 1, 1936; Alpine *Avalanche*, May 14, 1936; January 1, 1937; Yoakum *Herald*, November 10, 1938; Marshall *News-Messenger*, March 14, 1939.

39. Quoted in the Fort Worth *Star-Telegram*, August 24, 1937.

also found the Chisos Mountains "unworldly in their cragginess."[40]

The grandeur of the Big Bend inspired even those who had never seen it, which may account for the debatable quality but sincere effort of the following poem by Nolan Clark, self-proclaimed Texas Barber poet:[41]

> Come all you loyal Texans,
>   I've long been one myself,
> Let's rally round this project,
>   and take it off the shelf.
> Big Bend is on the program,
>   for our Nation's greatest park,
> With Uncle Sam our Captain,
>   we need not fear embark.

> This program is no "ballyhoo,"
>   no "gouger," "bleeder trick."
> With government endorsement,
>   we'll truly "make her stick."
> Artistically we'll landscape
>   her nature in the "raw"
> She'll be viewed with thrilling wonder
>   and with enchanting awe.
> She'll be our Nation's playground,
>   None ere surpass we know.
> She'll be a sound investment,
>   and double pay back "dough."

> With scenery fascinating,
>   balmy Southwest clime,
> She'll "magnetize" vacationist
>   with delight from time to time.
> The hunter and the fisherman,
>   here is their "paradise,"
> She's a sportsman's dreamland,
>   her winters have no ice.

---

40. Fort Worth *Star-Telegram*, October 24, 1937; Tyler *Morning Telegraph*, May 29, 1939; Albuquerque *Journal*, May 29, 1939; Corpus Christi *Caller-Times*, May 28, 1939; Dallas *Times-Herald*, May 30, 1939; NPS Press Release, August 13, 1939, File 501-03, Part II, BBNP, RG 79, NA; Amarillo *News*, April 15, 1939; Corpus Christi *Caller*, April 15, 1939; Shamrock *Texan*, April 15, 1939; San Angelo *Standard-Times*, April 7, 1939.

41. Clark's business slogan was "'Poemize' anything about anything." Clark to Tillotson, September 29, 1940, File 0-32, Part VIII, BBNP, RG 79, NA.

> So loyal Texans let's all "chip in,"
> Take Big Bend "on your lap"
> And show up to the World
> What's on our Lone Star Map.

One verse from fourteen year old Pete Williams from San Angelo, published in the employee's newsletter of the Texas State Parks Board, captured as well as words can the spell cast by the region:[42]

> The Big Bend's voice
>   is that of silence;
> Never a word has it spoken.
>   And its silence
> Has the power to still
>   even the memory of sound.
> The Big Bend is like a land
>   once known and then forgotten,
> Where modern machines and
>   evil ways have never come
> A land where legend
>   is stronger than truth.

National Geographic and *Literary Digest* were the only major magazines which featured articles on Big Bend before June 1944. While gathering material for a story, Frederick Simpich, an associate editor with the *Geographic*, claimed that he feasted on mountain lion meat, burro milk, and fried Spanish daggers. Simpich commented that the cougar flesh "looked and smelled like beef—but didn't taste like it." The author made several statements regarding the need for an international park, but most of his references to Big Bend depicted the area as a "waste of sun and silence" in which predators pillaged at will. The mountain lion which Simpich "feasted on," incidentally, was shot by a Mexican herdsman who recently had lost eighteen goats to the big cats.[43]

Life, Collier's, Saturday Evening Post, and *Parade* published

---

42. Pete Williams, "The Big Bend," *Sparks* (January, 1944), p. 5.

43. "Park for 'Texico': Big Bend International Reservation for Texas and Mexico," *Literary Digest*, March 21, 1936, p. 3; Fort Worth *Star-Telegram*, February 27, 1938; Frederick Simpich, "Down the Rio Grande: Taming this Strange, Turbulent Stream on Its Long Course from Colorado to the Gulf of Mexico," *National Geographic*, LXXVI (October, 1939), pp. 430, 439.

articles on the park after it was established in June 1944. Lesser known journals also carried features on the Big Bend region. The best of the major national publications was the *Life* pictorial essay. The Alpine *Avalanche* called it "probably the best piece of publicity ever given the Big Bend" and Newton B. Drury, Director of the NPS, likewise expressed praise for the magazine's work.[44]

The worst was Kenneth Foree's article in the *Saturday Evening Post*. Originally titled, "No Man's Land Becomes Park," it stressed the blood and gore of the region's past. When Foree asked Ross Maxwell for his critical comments, the superintendent of Big Bend responded that "It should be made clear that the Big Bend National Park is not an outlaw's paradise at the present." There were also numerous factual errors in Foree's article, but Maxwell fortunately caught most of them before the manuscript went to press. To Foree's credit, he detailed E. E. Townsend's significant contribution to the park movement.[45]

State-wide and local organizations contributed many hours of service, talent, and money to the Big Bend publicity campaign. Brewster County, which would greatly benefit from a national park, spent over $35,000 promoting Big Bend with parades, barbecues, tours, and other public relations activities. The Texas Federation of Women's Clubs conducted a very successful educational program to tell as many Texans as possible about Big Bend. The organization sent scores of letters to chambers of commerce, automobile associations, and travel bureaus. Club members also served as volunteer

---

44. "Big Bend, A Texas Wonderland is the Country's Newest National Park," *Life*, September 3, 1945, pp. 68–73; John Kord Lagemann, "Beauty on a Bend," *Collier's*, January 31, 1938, pp. 13–15, 67–68; "Big Bend is a National Park," *Parade*, March 28, 1948, pp. 19–21; Kenneth Foree, Jr., "Our New National Park on the Rio Grande," *Saturday Evening Post*, December 2, 1944, pp. 26–27, 106; Dee Woods, "The Dusty River Region," *South*, December, 1946, pp. 11, 23, 26; Tillotson, "Newest National Park—Big Bend," *National Motorist*, June, 1945, pp. 10, 17–18; Walter P. Taylor, "The Big Bend" (reprinted from *American Forests*, July, 1946), File 501-04, BBNP, RG 79, NA; Alpine *Avalanche*, September 7, 1945; Drury to P. P. Patraw, Tolson, and Herbert Evison, September 8, 1945, File 501-02, BBNP, RG 79, NA.

45. Foree to Maxwell, September 30, 1944, File 501-02, BBNP, RG 79, NA; Maxwell to Foree, October 5, 1944, File 501-02, BBNP, RG 79, NA. Isabelle F. Story, editor-in-chief of the NPS, harshly criticized Foree's article. She said, "Why not call it 'The Hard Men of Texas'? Big Bend seems incidental. And apparently the literary standards of the *Saturday Evening Post* are deteriorating." Story handwritten note, October 13, 1944, File 501-02, BBNP, RG 79, NA.

speakers throughout the state. The Texas Big Bend Park Association, Rotary International, Kiwanis, and the Lions were just a few of the other groups who lent support to the park movement.[46]

Although the extensive publicity campaign did not appreciably hasten the establishment of the park, it nevertheless helped project Big Bend from virtual obscurity into national prominence. Throughout the 1940s the region still was relatively inacessible to all but the hardy traveler who did not mind the dust, threat of flash floods, or quagmires of impassable mud. The wartime restrictions on travel kept the number of visitors down during the park's first couple of years, but the success of the promotional effort ultimately brought a substantial increase in the amount of tourists who went to Big Bend after the conclusion of the war. From 1944 through 1945 only 4,614 people visited the park, but more than 38,000 visitors came during the next two years. The annual visitation figures continued to rise throughout the following decades. It is foreseeable that one-half million annual visitors will be surpassed before the century is over.[47]

The publicity campaign for Big Bend National Park indicated that from the 1930s through World War II economic considerations dominated environmental attitudes at the local, state, and national levels. To be sure, there was pride in the area's biological and geological uniqueness and even provincial braggadocio concerning its rugged scenery, but the most convincing arguments centered on the economic benefits to be derived from tourism. Even Drew Pearson's opposition had economic overtones: the relatively inexpen-

---

46. Pecos *Enterprise*, April 8, 1938; Morelock to Drury, January 6, 1942, File 0-32, Part IX, BBNP, RG 79, NA; Marlin *Democrat*, May 23, 1939; Fort Worth *Star-Telegram*, March 7, 1939; May 21, 1939. Other organizations which helped publicize Big Bend and worked for its establishment were the Daughters of the American Revolution, Texas Federation of Garden Clubs, Texas Junior Chamber of Commerce, Texas Congress of Parents and Teachers, Zonta Club, Texas Real Estate Association, Cooperative Club, Texas Hotel Association, Texas Press Association, U. S. Highway 67 Association, Texas Club in New York City, International Parks Highway Association, as well as various other businesses, schools, and chambers of commerce.

47. Official Annual Visitation Figures, 1944–1972 (through June 30), July 27, 1972, Big Bend National Park Library. The "energy crisis" in late 1973 almost halved the number of visitors the following year—January through November 1973, 329,607; January through November 1974, 177,703. Visitation is now back to normal and has, on occasion, surpassed "pre-crisis" averages.

sive exploitation of candelilla wax for national defense. The positive position, although couched in different terms, was still an economic exploitation of sorts—this time of scenic and recreational resources. And economic priorities have persisted until the present day as the controversy over the wilderness proposal for the park aptly demonstrates.[48]

---

48. Donald C. Swain, "The National Park Service and the New Deal, 1933-1940," *Pacific Historical Review*, XLI (August, 1972), pp. 312-332, treats the historical development of the economic perspective in the National Park Service. Relevant chapters in John Ise, *Our National Park Policy: A Critical History* (Baltimore: Johns Hopkins Press, 1961), Alfred Runte, *National Parks: The American Experience* (Lincoln: University of Nebraska Press, 1979), and the concluding chapters of Nash's *Wilderness and the American Mind* show that economic rationalizations were not peculiar to the Big Bend park movement. Opposition to wilderness proposals that allegedly would restrict the development of visitor facilities in the park is documented in *Final Environmental Statement: Proposed Wilderness Classification; Big Bend National Park, Texas* (Washington, D. C.: United States Department of the Interior/National Park Service, 1975), *Wilderness Recommendation: Big Bend National Park, Texas* (Washington, D. C.: United States Department of the Interior/National Park Service, 1973), and *An Alternative to the Master Plan and Wilderness Proposal for Big Bend National Park* (Temple, Texas: Americans Backing Better Park Development, 1972).

V   The Ideal and the Reality

Park Service plans for the development of Big Bend National Park represent an interesting case study of the problems encountered when the park purpose of preservation and use confronts the reality of bureaucracy and American tourists. Even when closely supervised, the presence of people can easily alter or destroy the balance of nature. Except for overgrazing, the Big Bend area showed little evidence of human occupation and exploitation. Before the passage of the enabling legislation in 1935 the region's semi-arid character, lack of substantial mineral wealth, and rugged terrain had kept its population low.[1] The Service consequently had undeveloped lands in which it could utilize proven policies rather than follow the haphazard "trial and error" approach characteristic of earlier parks. It immediately proposed a thorough study of the natural, historic, scenic, and recreational values of Big Bend and a master plan which would help preserve the natural resources and provide enjoyment for present and future generations.[2]

---

1. There were numerous small claims in Big Bend but the only major mining activities were quicksilver operations at Terlingua and Study Butte and these were beyond the proposed park boundaries. "Report of the Big Bend Area, Texas," January, 1935, File 207, Records of Big Bend National Park, Record Group 79, National Archives Building (hereafter cited as BBNP, RG 79, NA). The population in Brewster County in the mid-1930s was 6,800 or about one person per square mile. "Report on the Proposed Big Bend National Park," March 3, 1934, File 207, BBNP, RG 79, NA.

2. "Report of the Big Bend Area, Texas," January, 1935, File 207, BBNP, RG 79, NA; NPS Press Release, March 3, 1935, File 0-32, Part I, BBNP, RG 79, NA; Bernard F. Manbey, "Proposed Big Bend National Park Report on Suggested Park Boundary, Engineering Requirements and General Notes," August 19, 1935, File 0-32, Part IX, BBNP, RG 79, NA; Victor H. Cahalane memorandum to Regional Directors, Regions I, II, and IV, December 8, 1944,

A few weeks after the passage of the enabling legislation a Service official visited the site of the proposed park. Commenting on deficiencies such as lack of good water, intense summer heat, shortage of development sites, and mediocre scenic qualities of the Rio Grande and Chisos Mountains, he suggested that the area had few redeeming features. And he concluded that until the proposed international park became a reality, Big Bend would remain "predominantly of local interest."[3]

George M. Wright, Chief of the Wildlife Division of the Service and a strong supporter of Big Bend, took issue with adverse criticism: "I feel that once an area has been given thorough study by the National Park Service and then recommended for park status, the submission of reports debating the question is not only wasteful but dangerous. . . . Our files, after all, are not confidential. Reports such as this . . . can be called in evidence against us at some time in the future."[4]

Wright's determination for consensus within the Park Service did not accurately portray the situation. Indeed, throughout the planning and development of Big Bend, ideological conflict of one sort or another existed between the national and regional offices, not to mention various divisions within the agency. Rather than a constructive dialogue which could have produced a master plan in conformity with national park ideals, contradictions and reversals of policy became commonplace. These developments not only alienated the general public and local boosters, but they also threatened the ecology of the Big Bend area.

Prior to 1933 the Service strongly encouraged Americans to visit their national parks. Since it was a relatively young agency, it hoped to convince Congress that the larger the numbers of visitors the greater the need for increased appropriations for protection and development. Various New Deal programs gave the Service the

---

File 204, BBNP, RG 79, NA.

    3. E. A. Pesonen, "Report on the Big Bend Proposed National Park," August 21, 1935, File O–32, Part I, BBNP, RG 79, NA. Pesonen was an assistant supervisor in the NPS. He had other criticisms in addition to the above. Pesonen cited a geologist who called the area "interesting but not unique" and a historian who said the Big Bend was "only of local significance historically."

    4. Wright memorandum to Conrad Wirth, September 5, 1935, File 0–32, Part II, BBNP, RG 79, NA.

opportunity to emphasize to communities near proposed and established national parks the economic advantages which result from federally funded projects and increased tourism.[5]

The Service especially utilized this economic approach to "sell" Big Bend to the people of the Lone Star State. To speed up land acquisition in the park, the Department of the Interior's Information Officer frequently issued news stories to remind Texans that the CCC was annually spending $100,000 in southern Brewster County, the site of the park. It also pointed out that the establishment of a national park would generate additional yearly expenditures of $225,000 for development, maintenance, and protection. By 1937 the Service estimate of the number of people who would visit Big Bend annually was set at 100,000 and the expenditure at $4,000,000. A decade later the forecast had risen to 240,000 visitors and by 1955 to half a million.[6]

These predictions created the impression that the Service intended to develop Big Bend extensively. In reality, the agency had no consistent policy and reacted instead to economic conditions and the recreational whims of the public. From 1933 through 1941, the Service received approximately $218,000,000 from New Deal emergency projects. These funds caused the agency to advocate a contradictory development program for Big Bend. One called for preserving and restoring the simple, primitive wilderness qualities of the area. The other advocated elaborate, complex, and expensive projects that would appeal to the anticipated hundreds of thousands of visitors to the "last frontier."[7]

An enthusiastic supporter of the paradoxical concept was Minor R. Tillotson, Southwestern Regional Director for the Park Service.

---

5. Donald C. Swain, "The National Park Service and the New Deal, 1933–1940," *Pacific Historical Review*, XLI (August, 1972), pp. 317, 327.

6. NPS Press Release, December 11, 1937, File 0–32, Part V, BBNP, RG 79, NA; San Antonio *Express*, September 12, 1938; Ward P. Webber memorandum to Thomas Vint, May 2, 1947, File 857, BBNP, RG 79, NA; Dedication Speech for Big Bend National Park by Douglas McKay, November 21, 1955, Big Bend National Park Library (hereafter cited as BBNP Lib). None of these estimates was at all accurate; for instance, in 1966 only 166,548 people came to the park. During the 1980s and 1990s the figures given for twenty years earlier should be realized.

7. Robert Shankland, *Steve Mather of the National Parks* (3rd ed.; New York: Alfred A. Knopf, 1970), p. 303.

In an address to a local booster group he expressed the hope that Big Bend would maintain its frontier atmosphere. Automobile roads would be held to a minimum. But the park would have an extensive network of horse and hiking trails. Tillotson proposed to "send the visitor on the hurricane deck of a cayuse instead of the rear seat of a limousine—give him chuck wagon instead of high hat hotel service—teach him to throw a diamond hitch and let him pack out on the trail from the [Chisos Basin] Window to Mariscal." The Regional Director closed his speech with an appeal "to make Big Bend utterly unique among the national parks."[8]

One suggestion for making the park "unique" was the idea of constructing a replica of Judge Roy Bean's Jersey Lilly saloon. The Big Bend region, incidentally, originally had been under Judge Bean's so-called jurisdiction—"The Law West of the Pecos." Fortunately, or otherwise, nothing came of the proposal to build this frontier institution.[9] Two further ideas to set Big Bend apart from other national parks concerned longhorn cattle and the possibility of an international park on the Rio Grande.

The Service planned to establish at Big Bend an old time cattle operation with dude ranch facilities for tourists. The project received an endorsement at one time or another from the wildlife chief, head of recreational planning, and assorted biologists and environmentalists in the Park Service as well as representatives from other cooperating agencies. First proposed in 1935, by the end of the decade the longhorn ranch seemed a definite fixture in Big Bend's development plans.[10]

---

8. Max Bentley, "Big Bend Park: Regional Executive Gets His First Look, Visions it as 'Utterly Different' Among National Parks," *West Texas Today* (October, 1940), p. 7.

9. E. R. Beck of Fort Worth first suggested the "Jersey Lilly" idea. Tillotson commented that it "may be well worth investigating." Tillotson to W. W. Thompson, December 22, 1942, File 620, BBNP, RG 79, NA.

10. J. D. Coffman, "Report on the Forest and Vegetative Aspect," August 9, 1935, File 0-32, Part I, BBNP, RG 79, NA; Maier to State Park ECW, attention of Wirth, October 30, 1935, File 0-32, Part II, BBNP, RG 79, NA; Wirth to Will C. Burnes, September 21, 1935, File 0-32 Part II, BBNP, RG 79, NA; Wright memorandum to Arthur Demaray, October 17, 1935, File 0-32, Part II, BBNP, RG 79, NA; W. B. McDougall, "Preliminary Report on a Plant Ecological Survey of the Big Bend Area," November 30, 1935, File 207, BBNP, RG 79, NA; Walter Prescott Webb to W. R. Hogan, September 5, 1937, Walter Prescott Webb

The Park Service justified the 200,000 acre ranch on historical, preservationist, and recreational grounds. The longhorn, the agency felt, had played as important a role in the West as had the buffalo. Both species were endangered but only the buffalo had begun to recover. Except for a few head of longhorns in the Wichita Mountains Game Preserve in Oklahoma, no extensive efforts to preserve this vestige of the open range cattle industry had ever been made. Hopefully, visitors could view a show herd of thirty to forty longhorns while approximately 400 others would be maintained for breeding purposes at Banta Shut-In, north of the Chisos Mountains and south of Tornillo Flat. Service officials maintained that the animals would not threaten the biological values of the Chisos Range and the ranch would serve "as a shrine for the preservation of the true spirit of the pioneer West." Entertainment for guests at the ranch would include spring and fall round-ups, brandings, and barbecues.[11]

Local ranchers were not particularly excited over the idea of the longhorn proposal. The Service had begun moving families and livestock out of the park during World War II in the midst of a public clamor to let them remain and help feed and clothe the allies. Livestock industry supporters argued that the park could not be developed until after the war and that the ranchers should be permitted to stay until hostilities had ended.[12] The Service contended that the over-grazed land could not support cattle, goats, or sheep in its depleted state and that it would take from twenty-five to 100 years before the range would return to its natural condition. In the meantime, the war years would provide an ideal time for the recovery process to begin. Obviously, the Service would have to exclude longhorns from Big Bend or else antagonize quite a few local

---

Papers, General Correspondence, 1937, Box 2M260, Barker Texas History Center, University of Texas at Austin.

11. "Report on the Field Investigation Together with Recommendations for the Establishment of a Boundary Line for the Big Bend National Park Project," September 9, 1935, File 0-32, Part II, BBNP, RG 79, NA; Maxwell and Borell, "Special Report: Longhorn Cattle Range Studies, Big Bend Area, Texas," June 10, 1937, File 0-32, Part IV, BBNP, RG 79, NA; Fort Worth *Star-Telegram*, August 8, 1938; "The Big Bend National Park Project, Texas," 1939, File 501, BBNP, RG 79, NA.

12. Pat McCarran to Harold Ickes, April 25, 1944, File 601, Part II, BBNP, RG 79, NA. McCarran was United States Senator from Nevada and a member of the Committee on Public Lands and Surveys.

people.[13]

Further developments in the 1940s ended any possibility of a longhorn ranch for Big Bend. The war forced many government agencies to "tighten their belts," the Park Service included. Costly programs such as the ranch and longhorn herds were either delayed or dropped altogether. Furthermore, Director Newton B. Drury opposed the plan because it would violate policies regarding the introduction of exotic species into parks. Those who tried to justify the longhorn's presence on historical grounds did not have a very strong case. J. Frank Dobie, for example, doubted if true representatives of the breed had ever roamed the Big Bend country.[14]

Tillotson was quite disappointed about the abandonment of the longhorn project. He felt the Chicago office had acted too hastily and had not given the regional office and the superintendent enough "leeway in presenting their own ideas and suggestions for the proposed park development before specific instructions were issued."[15] This conflict over development policies between the national and regional offices was to continue throughout the 1940s.

Of all the ideas to make Big Bend unique, the best suggestion concerned the establishment of an international park on the Rio Grande. The Park Service reported to President Roosevelt in 1935 that the "atmosphere in the region is decidedly one of *mañana*

---

13. Big Bend remained overgrazed throughout the time the longhorn proposal was discussed. A Park Service study found that fifty to one hundred acres would be required to sustain each longhorn and this was only after substantial recovery of the depleted range. W. B. McDougall, "Texas Longhorn Cattle: A Brief Report from the Point of View of Animal Husbandry," May 8, 1936, File 207, BBNP, RG 79, NA; Wirth to R. E. Thomason, March 10, 1944, File 900-01, BBNP, RG 79, NA; Walter P. Taylor, McDougall, and William B. Davis, "Preliminary Report of an Ecological Survey of Big Bend National Park, March-June, 1944," File 204, BBNP, RG 79, NA.

14. Additional evidence of the low priority the Park Service held can be seen by its removal in 1943 from Washington, D. C. to Chicago to make room for agencies directly concerned with the war effort. Drury memorandum to Regional Director, Region III, June 8, 1942, File 600-01, BBNP, RG 79, NA; Hillory Tolson memorandum to Regional Director, Region III, May 30, 1944, File 600-01, BBNP, RG 79, NA; Taylor, McDougall, and Davis, "Preliminary Report of an Ecological Survey of Big Bend National Park, March-June, 1944," File 204, BBNP, RG 79, NA; Dobie, *The Longhorns* (New York: Bramhall House, 1941).

15. Tillotson memorandum to Director, NPS, September 28, 1944, File 601-01, BBNP, RG 79, NA.

... this restful spirit in architecture and daily life ... rather than ruggedness should be the spirit of the day." Service architects drew up designs for a *hacienda* style lodge and tourist complex on the Rio Grande. Also included was a Mexican restaurant with waiters in native costume.[16]

Unfortunately, talks between Mexico and the United States regarding the proposed international park broke off in the late 1940s. Service planners realized that without an adjoining park on the Mexican side of the Rio Grande the location of the *hacienda* development would not suit Anglos. Most tourists arrived during the hot summer months and preferred to remain in the Chisos Mountains area where it was cooler. Temperatures along the river and near the international border often exceeded 110 degrees for several days at a time. Otherwise, the climate in this section of the park was ideal for vacationers for approximately eight months out of each year.[17]

In June 1944, Texas ceded jurisdiction of Big Bend and during the following month the federal government assumed control of its twenty-seventh national park. By this time the Service had a tentative master plan which represented a sound policy for restoring and maintaining the scenic, biological, geological, and historical resources as completely as possible. The three principal areas for physical developments were Panther Junction on the northeast slope of

---

16. "Report of the Big Bend Area, Texas," January, 1935, File 207, BBNP, RG 79, NA; Manbey, "Proposed Big Bend National Park Report on Suggested Park Boundary, Engineering Requirements and General Notes," August 19, 1935, File O–32, Part IX, BBNP, RG 79, NA; "The Big Bend National Park Project, Texas," 1939, File 501, BBNP, RG 79, NA; Tolson memorandum to Regional Director, Region III, May 30, 1944, File 601–01, BBNP, RG 79, NA; Tillotson, "Suggested Outline of Concessionaire Operations in Big Bend National Park," March 29, 1944, File 900–03, BBNP, RG 79, NA.

17. Concern about a central location in a future international park originally caused park planners to consider the river site for headquarters and the main tourist development. Oliver G. Taylor, "Comment on Big Bend National Park Master Plan," August 26, 1944, File 600–01, BBNP, RG 79, NA. The general manager of the organization that had the concessions operation at Big Bend said he was "particularly interested in the thought that the Mexican and southwestern atmosphere be maintained in this area." W. W. Thompson to Director, NPS, June 27, 1944, File 900–05, BBNP, RG 79, NA. Yet the concession restaurant failed in this regard for neither Texas nor Mexican specialties were served. Ross A. Maxwell memorandum to Regional Director, Region III, January 12, 1948, File 900–05, BBNP, RG 79, NA; "National Parks Concession, Inc. Schedule of Rates for 1949 Season," File 900–06, BBNP, RG 79, NA.

the Chisos Mountains, the old Daniels and Graham ranch on the Rio Grande near Boquillas, Mexico, and the Chisos Mountains Basin. In addition, a contract would be awarded to a concessioner to provide accommodations and services for visitors.

The Service selected Panther Junction as the site for park headquarters because of an adequate water supply, comfortable year-round climate, and its strategic location at the center of the park's road system. The principal visitor accommodations were a matter of much debate but eventually the river site at the Daniels and Graham ranch was selected. Here the Service planned to construct the main lodge as visitation increased and Congress would authorize the necessary funds.[18]

During the period when Big Bend was a state park the CCC established its headquarters in the Chisos Mountains Basin, where the enrollees constructed crude campsites, cabins, roads, and trails. The area had an elevation over 5,000 feet and soon became the principal summer tourist spot in the new national park. But despite increasing numbers of visitors, a 1948 Service report stressed that "development in this area will be restrained." Because of the relatively small area involved, extensive physical improvements "would seriously impair the scenic aspects . . . and depreciate its value as a visitor attraction." Moreover, it seemed doubtful that sufficient water resources were available for a large-scale tourist center. Nevertheless, Superintendent Ross A. Maxwell and Southwest Regional Director Tillotson persuaded Director Drury the next year to continue temporarily the development of the Basin so that there could be "good service in at least one area."[19] But by the mid-1950s the

---

18. Opinions as to the location of the main park development vacillated between the Chisos Basin and the Rio Grande. Generally, the national office favored the latter while the regional office and the superintendent supported the former.

19. "Big Bend National Park: Its Past—Its Future," September 20, 1948, File 501-04, BBNP, RG 79, NA. The following provide information on work done by the CCC: Fort Worth *Star-Telegram*, July 25, 1937; December 12, 1937; NPS Press Release, December 11, 1937, File 0-32, Part V, BBNP, RG 79, NA; Wirth memorandum to Regional Director, Region III, February 23, 1940, File 0-32, Part VIII, BBNP, RG 79, NA; Maxwell memorandum to Regional Director, Region III, June 20, 1949, Records of Newton B. Drury, Director's Personal File, Big Bend National Park, 1940 to March, 1951, RG 79, NA (hereafter cited as Drury File, BBNP, RG 79, NA).

so-called temporary facilities had become permanent, and the Basin was to remain the major tourist center in the park.

The main selling point of the Basin was that most of the visitation occurred during the summer months when the Rio Grande was quite hot. Conrad Wirth, one of the few in the national office who backed the Basin over the river development, suggested that "planners . . . spend a week down there [Rio Grande] during the hot summer days to determine whether it is a suitable climate for visitors." Maxwell estimated that ninety per cent of all visitors would come to the Basin and accommodations and services for them would be necessary. He opposed making the location a "sacred area" for "Ph.D.s to spend a vacation" since this would exclude most of the park's visitors. Based on his first-hand observations as superintendent, Maxwell did not feel that "we will be able to satisfy Texans with a ballroom, shade trees and Mexican music on the banks of the Rio Grande."[20]

The Secretary of the Interior awarded the franchise for Big Bend to National Park Concessions, Inc. It was a non-profit distributing corporation that operated in parks that were remote from large cities and considered poor business risks by private enterprise. Although Service officials had optimistically spoken of a thriving tourist trade for the area, they evidently did not take themselves too seriously. The federal government eventually constructed and retained the ownership of the buildings used by the concessioner. Following World War II, however, Congress failed to appropriate adequate funds for physical developments and National Park Concessions had to pay for the erection of temporary visitor facilities. These expenses, plus limited visitation, resulted in a loss to the company of $55,000 from 1946 to 1950.[21] One suggestion to minimize the

---

20. Tillotson memorandum to Director, NPS, July 11, 1945, File 900–05, BBNP, RG 79, NA; Wirth memorandum to Director, NPS, May 22, 1945, File 600–03, Part I, BBNP, RG 79, NA; Maxwell memorandum to Regional Director, Region III, May 7, 1945, File 600–03, Part I, BBNP, RG 79, NA; Tillotson memorandum to Director, NPS, November 11, 1944, File 718, BBNP, RG 79, NA.

21. Manley W. Allen to C. L. Andrews, April 26, 1948, File 900–02, BBNP, RG 79, NA; Demaray to Thomason, January 30, 1946, File 900–05, BBNP, RG 79, NA; Tolson memorandum to Regional Director, Region III, June 9, 1944, File 900–02, BBNP, RG 79, NA; Chris E. Taylor memorandum to Director, NPS, May 12, 1949, File 900–06, BBNP, RG 79, NA; Demaray memorandum to Re-

problem was to close concessions in the Chisos Basin from November through April when there were few visitors in the park. But Superintendent Maxwell opposed the idea because the Service had promised the people of Texas year-round recreational facilities.[22]

Tillotson had consistently emphasized that the Big Bend was "to be essentially a saddle and pack horse area," but lack of funds for the saddle horse concession and for developing trails prevented the realization of these objectives until August 1949. Their addition considerably stimulated the concessions operation. Superintendent Maxwell noted that by 1952 the horse riding concession business had increased by 300 per cent. Big Bend's interpretive programs also suffered because of the lack of adequate congressional appropriations for national parks. Not until May 1947 was the first campfire program given and throughout the 1940s the park did not have a naturalist.[23]

Through the 1950s and early 1960s the number of tourists to Big Bend averaged only 80,000 annually, a figure far below the estimated 240,000. Although this was about one-tenth of the amount that other Western parks experienced, the concession franchise no longer operated at a deficit and all talk of closing some of the facilities for part of the year had long since ceased. In fact, cabins and campsites were frequently filled to capacity during the Christmas and Easter seasons.[24]

---

gional Director, Region III, September 12, 1949, Drury File, BBNP, RG 79, NA.

22. Maxwell memorandum to Regional Director, Region III, June 20, 1949, Drury File, BBNP, RG 79, NA; Tillotson memorandum to Director, NPS, July 11, 1949, Drury File, BBNP, RG 79, NA; Demaray to H. S. Sanborn, August 4, 1949, Drury File, BBNP, RG 79, NA; Demaray memorandum to Regional Director, Region III, August 4, 1949, Drury File, BBNP, RG 79, NA; Sanborn to Demaray, September 5, 1949, Drury File, BBNP, RG 79, NA.

23. Tillotson memorandum to Director, NPS, April 28, 1942, File 600-03, Part I, BBNP, RG 79, NA; Maxwell, "History of Big Bend National Park" (ms), 1952, BBNP Lib; Maxwell memorandum to Regional Director, Region III, November 6, 1947, File 900-05, BBNP, RG 79, NA; "Superintendent's Monthly Narrative Report, May, 1947," June 6, 1947, File 207-02.3, BBNP, RG 79, NA; Maxwell memorandum to Director, NPS, May 28, 1947, File 204, BBNP, RG 79, NA.

24. Official Annual Visitation Figures, 1944-1972 (through June 30), July 27, 1972, BBNP Lib. From 1950 to 1962 annual visitation to Big Bend ranged from 67,000 to approximately 91,100. Beginning in 1963, visitation increased at a rapid rate. The Park Service does not offer any "precise explanation" for this, but

Meanwhile, the Service's limited budget and the temporary decline in visitors because of gasoline and tire rationing during World War II did more to preserve the "last frontier" and "unspoiled wilderness" of the Big Bend than any planning proposals. The park's isolation and its primitive accommodations discouraged all but the most adventurous vacationers. State and local boosters who supported the park largely because of expected economic returns were obviously disappointed. But on the positive side, the natural and historic resources remained stable.[25]

In this latter respect, other national parks generally did not fare as well as Big Bend. Conrad Wirth, Director of the Park Service from 1951 to 1964, wrote in a 1966 *National Geographic* article about the degenerating conditions in the parks since the early 1940s: "Facilities were out of date and run down, roads were in dangerous conditions, trails were washed out, employee morale was at a low level, and even scenic beauty was deteriorating."[26]

The post-war American public had literally "loved to death" its national park system. It could adequately accommodate 21,000,000 people, yet it faced an annual onslaught of 55,000,000. The Service budget had remained inadequate to meet the increased usage thanks largely to the Cold War mentality and increasing military expenditures. In response to the crisis, in 1955 the Park Service presented President Dwight Eisenhower and Congress with a long-range package plan—Mission 66, which stated that present and future needs

---

the country's growing awareness of wilderness no doubt contributed significantly to this trend. Even the high price of gasoline following the so-called energy crisis in late 1973 and early 1974 only temporarily reduced visitation. A year later it was back to its "pre-crisis" level, or approximately 300,000+. In the 1980s, however, annual visitation has dropped to 200,000+ with 60,000 of these coming during March and April of each year.

25. Although Park Service experts debated the extent of the range recovery, none doubted that there had been noticeable improvement since the cessation of grazing in 1945. See File 718, BBNP, RG 79, NA. With the establishment of the park and the subsequent curtailment of hunting and trapping, Big Bend's deer, panther, coyote, javelina, beaver, quail, and dove populations increased. Maxwell memorandum to Director, NPS, October 5, 1945, File 720-04, BBNP, RG 79, NA. An examination of the "Annual Animal Census Reports," "Biennial Animal Census Reports," and "Wildlife Inventories" in the BBNP Library also reveals a relative stability of wildlife populations.

26. Wirth, "The Mission Called 66," *National Geographic*, CXXX (July, 1966), p. 11.

of the national parks would cost $786,500,000 over a ten year period. Both the president and Congress responded favorably to the idea. The program for physical improvements, restoration of park resources, increased staffs for protection and interpretation, and additional lands to round out the system would eventually cost the American taxpayer over a billion dollars.[27]

Big Bend alone received $14,000,000 from Mission 66 to improve roads, bridges, trails, and tourist accommodations. The major visitor facilities included a lodge, restaurant, cabins, and campsites in the Basin. A Texas newspaper editor remarked that the extensive developments "will neither sissify nor citify the wilderness which is the principal appeal of all national parks. It will bring the wilderness a little nearer to the average visitor, help him understand it and enjoy it without risk to his health and safety, and keep down the wear and tear on the car in which he will travel."[28] The editor, however, did not mention the "wear and tear" on the ecology of the Big Bend.

The 1960s witnessed a large influx of visitors to the park and healthy revenues for West Texas communities. At the very time that the long promised economic returns were finally becoming a reality, the balance of nature in the Chisos Basin and elsewhere in the park was greatly endangered by the increasing flood of people. Thus, in 1971, the Park Service prepared another master plan that recommended the designation of 533,900 acres of Big Bend lands as "wilderness," or roughly seventy-five per cent of the entire area. Wilderness classification, incidentally, means the absence of public use roads and developed campgrounds and picnic facilities.[29]

---

27. *Ibid.*, pp. 11, 15–16. A good "insider's" view of the Park Service is William C. Everhart, *The National Park Service* (New York: Praeger Publishers, 1972).

28. Presley Bryant, State Editor for the Fort Worth *Star-Telegram*, quoted in Virginia Madison, *The Big Bend Country of Texas* (2nd ed.; New York: October House, 1968), p. 249.

29. The following definition of wilderness is from the 1964 congressional act creating a national wilderness preservation system: "an area where the earth and its community of life are untrammeled by man, where man himself is a visitor who does not remain . . . an area of undeveloped Federal land retaining its primeval character and influence, without permanent improvements or human habitation, which is protected and managed so as to preserve its natural conditions . . . " U. S., *Statutes at Large*, LXXVIII, p. 891; *Wilderness Study: Big Bend*

The master plan suggested that visitor use of the Basin should be limited and that overnight accommodations there should eventually be excluded. Also, the horse riding concession in the Basin should be moved, and Rio Grande Village should become the park's major tourist development. A secondary visitor-use area would be Castolon, southeast of Santa Elena Canyon. In addition, the plan encouraged more use of the desert areas and the building of tourist lodging and trailer campsites outside of the park to help relieve Big Bend of the masses that formerly headquartered in the Chisos Mountains.[30]

A public hearing in Alpine, Texas in January 1972 brought determined opposition to the master plan and wilderness recommendation. Moreover, the Travel Department of the Texas Highway Department, the Texas Tourist Development Agency, and Governor Preston Smith were against the proposals. The only state agency to support the recommendations was the Texas Parks and Wildlife Department. The principal spokesman for local sentiment was Johnny Newell, who headed the Big Bend National Parks Development Committee. Newell agreed with some points of the master plan but rejected the wilderness recommendation because of its ban on public roads in seventy-five per cent of the park. He argued that a greater use of the desert area would hardly be possible without more convenient access than foot trails.[31]

Although the 1964 Wilderness Act expressly did not "modify

National Park (Washington, D. C.: Department of the Interior/National Park Service, 1971), p. 20. The final environmental statement provides for the potential wilderness classification of an additional 25,700 acres, or roughly seventy-nine per cent of the total park acreage. *Big Bend National Park: Final Environmental Statement; Proposed Wilderness Classification* (Washington, D. C.: Department of the Interior/National Park Service, 1975), p. 1. Background on the Wilderness Act can be found in Michael McCloskey, "The Wilderness Act of 1964: Its Background and Meaning," *Oregon Law Review*, XLV (1966), pp. 288–321.

    30. *Big Bend National Park Master Plan: Preliminary Draft* (Washington, D. C.: Department of the Interior/National Park Service, 1971).

    31. Later, other state agencies, some of which had not been contacted in 1972, voiced support for the wilderness proposal. These included the Historical Commission, Department of Agriculture, Industrial Commission, Water Quality Board, Air Control Board, Water Rights Commission, and the Highway Department's engineering division. The Texas Tourist Development Agency continues to oppose the proposal. *Big Bend National Park: Final Environmental Statement* pp. 131–132, 153–170; Odessa *American*, January 16, 1972.

the statutory authority under which units of the National Park System are created," several Texans felt otherwise. State Representative Hilary Doran, Jr. from Del Rio and State Senator W. E. Snelson from Midland noted that Big Bend National Park was a gift of the people of the Lone Star State to the federal government. It was turned over with the understanding that it could be used by all of the people, not just by a backpacking minority. Richard H. Pierce, manager of the Travel Department of the Texas Highway Department, expressed the same opinion. The wilderness recommendation would place most of Big Bend "off limits for casual family travelers . . . off limits for the station wagon family with youngsters, who are neither inclined nor equipped for crosscountry hiking and dry-camp survival . . . off limits for the senior citizens who travel so extensively, but are physically incapable of the rigors of backpacking across mountain and desert."[32]

Carter "Buck" Newsome, a former Texas Ranger and operator of the saddle horse concession in the Basin, regarded the master plan and wilderness recommendation as something "cooked up" by a "bunch of ecology nuts [who] think the horses are ruining that part of the park." Newsome opposed moving his concession to Rio Grande Village because a "dude can't survive in the kind of temperature that we have on the desert during the summer. . . . They would faint and fall over the minute they stepped outside their air conditioned cabins."[33]

Newsome's protests apparently had some effect. The revised master plan, published after the public hearing, recommended that the horse concession "be relocated to a suitable site out of the Basin" and suggested Ceniza Flat, a mid-elevation site four miles below Panther Junction which was accessible to the mountains but not subjected to the harsh summer temperatures of the Rio Grande Village site. Another compromise in the revised plan relegated Rio Grande Village from *the* major park visitor-use development to only *a* major development. Ceniza Flat was to be the "safety valve" to take pressure off of the Basin. Also, overnight accommodations would remain

---

32. Ibid.; *Wilderness Study: BBNP*, p. 18; *Wilderness Recommendation: Big Bend National Park, Texas* (Washington, D. C.: Department of the Interior/National Park Service, 1973), Appendix, Hearing Officer's Report.

33. Odessa *American*, January 16, 1972.

in the Basin.[34]

The vocal minority who opposed the master plan and wilderness recommendation did so largely for economic reasons. A spokesman for the ecology groups supporting the proposals criticized the opposition for having "selfish, commercial interests." The charge was not altogether fair for groups such as Newell's Big Bend Development Committee wanted only what the Park Service had repeatedly promised—a prosperous tourist industry for West Texas. Not surprisingly, every city, chamber of commerce, and county in the vicinity of the national park unanimously disapproved of the wilderness recommendation. Many of the opponents of the wilderness proposal felt the Park Service had capably managed Big Bend and questioned the conversion of much of the area into an undeveloped wilderness. Apparently they were of the opinion that the Service would continue to build roads and construct visitor accommodations throughout the park.[35]

The Park Service can be criticized for its ambivalent development policies and its exaggerated visitation predictions for Big Bend, but the agency never advocated a large-scale physical improvements program for the entire park area. In the 1980s the principal park roads and sites for visitor facilities are basically the same as those proposed in the 1940s. The furor raised at the public hearing indicated that the Park Service has successfully publicized the economic reasons for a national park. In doing so, it failed to impress upon state and local people the significance of ecological, recreational, and inspirational justifications for wilderness.[36] Nevertheless, the policy

---

34. *Big Bend National Park Master Plan* (Washington, D. C.: Department of the Interior/National Park Service, 1973), pp. 20–21; *BBNP Master Plan: Preliminary Draft*, pp. 21–23.

35. *Odessa American*, January 16, 1972; *Wilderness Recommendation: BBNP*, Appendix, Hearing Officer's Report. Area chambers of commerce, cities, the West Texas Council of Governments, and other local organizations are steadfast in their opposition to the wilderness proposal and "that the development of the area should *not* be absolutely and irrevocably frozen by an act of congress." See Dorothy L. McBride, Mayor of Alpine, to Bill Rabenstein, Chief Park Naturalist, BBNP, March 4, 1974 and Newell to Robinstein (*sic*), March 1, 1974 in *BBNP: Final Environmental Statement*, pp. 172–177.

36. After 1966 acceleration of the Southeast Asian conflict put a stop to the ample federal funds the Park Service had received during Mission 66. In fact funds for visitor-use improvements have declined $30,000,000 annually. For

should bring about the gradual recovery of the park's flora and fauna.

---

example, in Service needed $1,800,000,000 for physical improvements, yet only received $40,000,000. Everhart, *The National Park Service*, p. 239.

VI   Ranchers and Predators

The National Park Service realizes the possibility of confrontation with local ranchers each time Congress authorizes a new park. In the mid-1940s a rancher wrote to the park superintendent that he considered Big Bend National Park a "curse" on the livestock industry of Texas. He regarded it as a "breeding ground" for predatory animals who sneaked from their sanctuary, slaughtered the neighboring sheep, goats, and cattle, and then returned to the safety of the national park. In retaliation, the irate rancher admitted that he permitted his cows and horses to graze illegally on the park's already depleted grasses. "You keep all your preditory (*sic*) animals within your park boundaries, and I will keep all my livestock from entering the Park," he told the Park Service.[1]

Some stockmen opposed Big Bend because of the approximately 700 thousand acres that were removed from the tax rolls. But when they found out that the county would lose only about $4,200, their criticism subsided. Another area of strife concerned the argument that thousands of acres of land which could feed and clothe the allies during World War II was closed to domestic livestock. But the most persistent opposition continued over the issue of predators in the park. Park Service policy dictates that all wildlife receive protection, including the large flesh eating animals. Such a principle ran counter to the rancher's protective instinct for the safety of his livestock. His usual reaction was to destroy as many predators as possible. Occasionally the stockmen succeeded so well they completely eradicated some species, one being the wolf. In other instances, their efforts

---

1. G. A. Morriss to Ross A. Maxwell, August 18, 1946, File 900–01, Records of Big Bend National Park, Record Group 79, National Archives Building (hereafter cited as BBNP, RG 79, NA).

had little effect, as in the case of the coyote.[2]

The first permanent cattlemen entered the Big Bend country after the Civil War and encountered numerous predators, but only the lobo wolf seriously threatened their herds. The ranchers systematically battled the lobo by poisoning, trapping, and shooting. The lone survivor was killed in Pecos County in West Texas in the early twentieth century. Other predators like mountain lions, black bears, coyotes, bobcats, and golden eagles likewise abounded. But since they did not really endanger cattle, ranchers merely killed them for sport.[3]

Sheep and goat raisers came to the Big Bend about the same time as the cattlemen, but their numbers did not increase to significant proportions until the outbreak of World War I. The global confrontation produced ready markets for all types of agricultural products. Shortly after its conclusion, many ranchers left the Big Bend country because of the agricultural recession, drought, and poison weeds that devastated their flocks. In the 1920s they returned in force, and since sheep and goats were prey for all of the big carnivores, the battle against predators now began in earnest. Private individuals employed their own trappers, one of whom destroyed 121 panthers and three bears in the Big Bend area between 1932 and 1945. The first government trapper began work in 1937.[4]

The golden eagle was especially anathema to sheep and goat raisers. This elusive bird was difficult to trap and unless surprised on the ground feeding on a carcass, nearly impossible to shoot. In desperation, ranchers hired pilots and planes, organized eagle clubs, and for one hundred dollars a year bought protection from this predator. The state and county also paid some of the expenses for eradication.

---

2. Maxwell, "History of Big Bend National Park" (ms), 1952, Big Bend National Park Library (hereafter cited as BBNP Lib); Conrad Wirth to Regional Officer, Region III, June 2, 1937, File O-32, Part IV, BBNP, RG 79, NA. The coyote has proven to be the most immune to predator control efforts. Attempts to destroy this species seem to cause it to thrive. Recently the coyote has appeared in Maine. See John N. Cole, "The Return of the Coyote," *Harper's Magazine*, CCXLVI (May, 1973), pp. 48–51.

3. Maxwell memorandum to Regional Director, Region III, April 16, 1948, File 719, BBNP, RG 79, NA.

4. *Ibid.*; J. O. Langford with Fred Gipson, *Big Bend: A Homesteader's Story* (Austin: University of Texas Press, 1955), p. 153.

Between 1930 and 1942 one pilot spent approximately 1,400 hours in the air and claimed to have killed 2,500 eagles in the Big Bend region.[5]

Another source of the stockmen's discontent was the realization that with the final establishment of Big Bend in June 1944, grazing rights in the park would cease. The Service did not actively begin to enforce the policy until one year later, and the small staff intensified its efforts throughout 1946. In 1947 the NPS imported the first pronghorned antelope into Big Bend as part of of a plan to restock the native fauna of the area. Rumors circulated among ranchers that the agency had also brought in wolves from Arizona. The stockmen's fears appeared confirmed when one of their number claimed he had trapped a lobo, while several others reported actually having seen employees releasing carnivores inside the park boundaries.[6]

The possibility that Big Bend National Park would become a "breeding ground" for predators, especially coyotes, golden eagles, wolves, and mountain lions, incensed the ranchers. One claimed to have killed more than a hundred panthers in the Big Bend area during a ten year period. An editorial in the *Sheep and Goat Raisers Magazine*, the organ for West Texas sheep and goat interests, called Big Bend "the most perfect incubator of predatory animals in the United States today." The journal stated that a rancher whose property bordered the park employed one man full time trapping predators. Over a period of a few months he claimed to have captured eighty panthers.[7]

Stories about the mountain lion and other predators added fuel to the controversy. Sam Nail, who had raised cattle and horses in the Big Bend country since 1909, told a *National Geographic* writer in 1938 that in the three decades he had lived there, cougars had killed 600 of his horses and cattle. Another story concerned a round-up of

---

5. Virginia Madison, *The Big Bend Country of Texas* (2nd ed.; New York: October House, 1968), p. 151.

6. "Annual Animal Census Report for Big Bend National Park, 1950," BBNP Lib; El Paso *Herald-Post*, December 3, 1947; San Angelo *Standard-Times*, December 7, 1947; December 14, 1947; E. E. Townsend to Maxwell, December 17, 1947, File 719, BBNP, RG 79, NA.

7. San Angelo *Standard-Times*, December 14, 1947; "The Big Bend Park Incubator," *Sheep and Goat Raisers Magazine*, February, 1948 (typed copy of editorial in File 719, BBNP, RG 79, NA).

1,000 mares in 1947 near the Chisos Mountains at which time only one colt was in the entire herd. The ranchers surmised that panthers were to blame, since they supposedly delighted in killing helpless and weak animals. Similar tales recorded the cowardly nature of the lion. One told of a puma who consistently avoided encounters with a foe of equal strength. Yet on a single night it purportedly slaughtered seventeen sheep, much more than it could possibly eat. The theme of "bad" versus "good" animals was accepted by many without question. The caption of a photograph in the San Angelo *Standard-Times* of two dead cougars stated that they "had their last lamb just a short time before they were caught and slain." The accompanying article commented that the mountain lion regarded the lamb, long a symbol of innocence and purity, as a "preferred delicacy."[8]

The golden eagle likewise had horror stories attributed to it. One witness told of watching the bird land on the back of a full grown sheep. As the terrified animal desperately ran about, the eagle, while holding on with one talon, slit the victim's throat with the other. The Park Service inadvertently added to the eagle's reputation with a press release that depicted the bird as a "destructive outlaw." The writer commented that the eagle's depredations, however, were "far outweighed by the beneficial results in maintaining the balance of nature through his preying upon gophers, jackrabbits, and other rodents and parasites that are destructive to agriculture." The average rancher was not particularly impressed and considered the eagle a villain who should be destroyed.[9]

Essential to the livestock industry's case against that of the Park Service was the firm belief that the Big Bend really was a "breeding ground" for predators. According to one theory, the pro-

---

8. Frederick Simpich, "Down the Rio Grande: Tracing this Strange, Turbulent Stream on its Long Course from Colorado to the Gulf of Mexico," *National Geographic*, LXXVI (October, 1939), p. 430; San Angelo *Standard-Times*, December 14, 1947; January 28, 1948.

9. San Angelo *Standard-Times*, January 28, 1948; NPS Press Release, May 8, 1937, File 0-32, Part IV, BBNP, RG 79, NA. One Park Service official wrote the following about the press release: "This is about the worst eagle story I have yet seen and I've heard of them eating babies by the dozen!"[BHT] Ben H. Thompson to[Connie] Conrad Wirth (no date), File 0-32, Part IV, BBNP, RG 79, NA.

hibition against grazing forced flesh eating animals to hunt domestic stock on private range lands beyond the park's boundaries. At the same time, they could find sanctuary in the park. The ranchers argued that the protection offered by the park caused an unnatural increase in predators and a corresponding rise in the number of victims. Another theory blamed the increasingly large deer population outside Big Bend on panthers which had purportedly forced them out of the park and onto adjacent grazing lands. When the big cats followed, they were not particular where their meal came from.[10]

Late in 1947 the sheep and goat interests of West Texas felt that the predator problem had reached crisis proportions. They consequently sought the services of J. Frank Dobie in hopes that the internationally known author and storyteller could persuade the federal government to authorize a trapper to work within Big Bend National Park. Although a university professor, Dobie still had strong attachments to the cattle business. When Dobie accepted an invitation to give a talk before the West Texas Historical and Scientific Society, representatives for both the NPS and the ranchers attended.

Dobie delivered a typical rambling address, but one portion specifically concerned the Big Bend livestock interests. He said that they were no different from the Boston manufacturers, since both desired government subsidies and a high tariff to give them more than their just due for their products. According to Dobie, the ranchers wanted federal money to clear their lands of prickly pear plants, build water tanks, and dig wells. And now they also demanded trappers maintained at federal expense inside the park itself. Dobie lashed out at the sheep and goat men as a group that "criminally mined the soil" so that after ten years the land was worth less than a dime an acre.[11] After the talk, no more was heard of the plan to enlist him as a spokesman for livestock interests.

Ranchers still had several alternative courses of action to alleviate what they felt was a very serious crisis. At their annual convention in El Paso in December 1947 the Texas Sheep and Goat Raisers Association passed resolutions calling for more federal funds for predatory animal control, an alliance with cattlemen to combat

---

10. San Angelo *Standard-Times*, December 14, 1947; January 28, 1948.

11. Maxwell memorandum to Regional Director, Region III, February 1, 1948, File 719, BBNP, RG 79, NA.

the common foe, and the right to follow the "hot" trail of a depredating animal into the park. In addition, the organization reiterated its position that the NPS not permit Big Bend to become a "breeding ground" for carnivores, nor should the Park Service import dangerous wildlife. Vestal Askew, secretary of the Association, sent a copy of the resolutions to the NPS.[12]

Arthur Demaray, Acting Director of the Park Service, replied in January 1948 and assured the members of the Association that the Service had never imported a predator to Big Bend National Park and had no plans of doing so in the future. The Acting Director also stated the Park Service's belief that the reputed increase in large carnivores was more exaggeration than fact. To support this contention, he explained that if Big Bend had as many predators as the ranchers claimed, there would not be such an abundance of deer, both in and out of the park. Demaray concluded that the NPS, through Big Bend's Superintendent Ross A. Maxwell, would work out "measures for safe-guarding the interests of the ranchers" from predators which originated in the national park. But, he added, hunting was "strictly prohibited by law" and this in no way included permitting hunters to trail predators into the park.[13]

Demaray's letter did little to allay the fears of the ranchers, or improve relations with them. He had refuted the stockmen's arguments with circumstantial evidence rather than statistical data largely because an accurate study had never been made by a park naturalist.[14] But his remark that the ranchers had exaggerated the number of predators in Big Bend left him open to the charge that the Park Service underestimated their strength. Also, Demaray had not offered any concrete proposals as to exactly what the Park Service would do to protect the interests of the ranchers. They were now determined to pursue another course.

In the February issue of *Sheep and Goat Raisers Magazine*, H. M. Phillips stated that West Texas ranchers were not opposed to

---

12. Askew to Director, NPS, December 22, 1947, File 719, BBNP, RG 79, NA; "Superintendent's Monthly Narrative Report, December, 1947," January 8, 1948, File 207-02.3, BBNP, RG 79, NA.

13. Demaray to Askew, January 19, 1948, File 719, BBNP, RG 79, NA.

14. P. P. Patraw to Superintendent, BBNP, January 23, 1948, File 719, BBNP, RG 79, NA.

Big Bend as a vacation spot or wildlife refuge. In fact, "some of the most enthusiastic boosters of the Big Bend" were ranchmen, but they remained very much against the park's use as an "unhampered breeding ground."[15]

An editorial in the same issue of the magazine contradicted Phillips's statement in regard to the ranchers's support of Big Bend. It stated that the park contained "some of the most worthless land in the country" and implied that the well publicized scenery was hardly worth the arduous trip required before one could view the so-called splendor. The editorial indicated no awareness of Demaray's letter and noted that NPS officials had not denied the allegations that they were importing carniverous animals, or that Big Bend was a "predator incubator." Park Service officials realized a rebuttal to the charges in the magazine would probably accomplish nothing since Askew, an executive of the Texas Sheep and Goat Raisers Association, apparently had disregarded Demaray's explanation of his agency's policy. Instead, the Service merely relied on Superintendent Maxwell's skills with the local people at explaining and implementing NPS programs.[16]

When the controversy began to develop in December 1947, Maxwell immediately visited the neighboring ranches and towns to determine attitudes of the local residents toward the park as a "predator incubator."[17] He found several prominent ranchers who believed that no increase had occurred in the predator population since the establishment of the park. One even considered Big Bend National Park among "the best things that ever happened to Brewster County." Another noted that if carniverous animals had indeed multiplied as much as the Association's magazine indicated, the number of deer should have decreased in the park. He further

---

15. El Paso *Times*, February 17, 1948.

16. "The Big Bend Incubator," *Sheep and Goat Raisers Magazine*, February, 1948 (typed copy of editorial in File 719, BBNP, RG 79, NA); Newton B. Drury memorandum to Regional Director, Region III,. March 15, 1948, File 719, BBNP, RG 79, NA; Patraw memorandum to Director, NPS, April 30, 1948, File 719, BBNP, RG 79, NA.

17. "Superintendent's Monthly Narrative Report, November, 1947," December 5, 1947, File 207–02.3, BBNP, RG 79, NA; "Superintendent's Monthly Narrative Report, January, 1948," February 4, 1948, File 207–02.3, BBNP, RG 79, NA; Maxwell memorandum to Regional Director, Region III, December 23, 1947, File 719, BBNP, RG 79, NA.

stated that he would not go out of his house at night if hundreds of panthers lurked in the shadows, according to some stories. Maxwell made a special effort to talk to the individual who had supposedly trapped eighty cougars in a few months time. He told the superintendent that the magazine reporter misquoted—he had said "eight,' and not "eighty."[18]

Others, however, felt predators had substantially increased. A personal friend of Maxwell's laid the blame directly on the park and said that he favored a government trapper. Another who owned land adjacent to Big Bend indicated that he intended to remain a good neighbor, but he firmly believed that the park had caused a rise in the predator population.[19]

Maxwell also interviewed several private and government trappers and game wardens and learned that the lobo purportedly caught was a large, dark coyote called a "chihuahua wolf." Most of those he talked with felt that the number of predators had not increased. Ray Williams, captain of the West Texas game wardens and the man who supposedly had bagged the 2,500 eagles previously mentioned, considered the protests of the sheep and goat men as a "bunch of nonsense" and doubted if they could prove their charges. Based on his extensive investigation, Maxwell concluded that two or three panthers on a single ranch would be an extraordinary number. Moreover, on several ranches there had been no signs of panther whatsoever, and most had not been bothered by predators to any significant degree.[20]

The sheep and goat men eventually realized that radical proposals such as demanding a trapper within the park's boundaries would not help curb the alleged increase of predators. The Park Service definitely would not permit hunting and trapping and other violations of established NPS policy. Consequently, in June 1948 an executive committee of the Sheep and Goat Raisers Association

---

18. Maxwell memorandum to Regional Director, Region III, January 23, 1948, File 719, BBNP, RG 79, NA; Maxwell memorandum to Regional Director, Region III, April 16, 1948, File 719, BBNP, RG 79, NA.

19. Maxwell memorandum to Regional Director, Region III, January 23, 1948, File 719, BBNP, RG 79, NA.

20. Maxwell memorandum to Regional Director, Region III, April 16, 1948, File 719, BBNP, RG 79, NA.

met in Uvalde and approved a resolution which petitioned the NPS to appropriate funds for trappers and hunters to patrol the park's perimeter and protect the adjoining ranches from "reinfestation" of mountain lions, coyotes, bobcats, and wolves. The measure stated that the ranchers themselves had spent considerable money eradicating predators. According to the stockmen, those animals that were causing the trouble clearly came from the national park.[21]

Park Service officials regarded the latest resolution from the ranchers as indicative that the furor over Big Bend's predators was subsiding. The conciliatory nature of the measure encouraged Hillory Tolson of the NPS to express his appreciation to Ernest Williams, the new secretary of the Association, for the request to limit trappers to the exterior of the park. Tolson referred to Maxwell's investigative efforts which had revealed that mountain lions and bobcats were comparatively rare, wolves were nonexistent, but that coyotes had become more numerous. Due to the large quantity of small game present in the park, Tolson felt they would remain close to their food source. The Park Service official concluded that the evidence gathered indicated that the park's predators did not constitute a serious problem for the adjacent landowners.[22]

The ranchers still remained skeptical and in January 1949 requested the Fish and Wildlife Service in the Department of the Interior to study the predator problem in Big Bend National Park. The action infuriated the Park Service hierarchy and Director Newton B. Drury wrote to the head of the sister agency to remind him that "investigations of park problems are made only on request of the National Park Service." Nevertheless, Drury did permit the Fish and Wildlife Service to conduct a survey the following February.[23]

Ross Maxwell personally guided the investigators through the park and especially looked for signs of coyote. But after a thorough search, the Fish and Wildlife men concluded that both bobcats and coyotes were by no means abundant, and the number of coyotes in Big Bend constituted only one-tenth of those found outside the

---

21. Maxwell to the author, August 6, 1973; Ernest Williams to Demaray, June 28, 1948, File 719, BBNP, RG 79, NA.

22. Tolson to Williams, July 15, 1948, File 719, BBNP, RG 79, NA.

23. Director, NPS memorandum to Director, Fish and Wildlife Service, January 25, 1949, File 719, BBNP, RG 79, NA.

park. The investigators did find ample evidence of panthers, but as long as the deer population remained stable they did not regard them as an immediate menace. Although not a serious threat to the ranches north of the park at the moment, the future could be a different story. Finally, Fish and Wildlife officials recommended that Maxwell should attend Sheep and Goat Raisers' meetings to improve relations between the Park Service and the livestock interests.[24]

Maxwell followed the advice. In 1952, his last year as superintendent, he wrote that "the public relations between the park and all outside organizations has improved and I am sure that the present status is much better that it was in 1944 and 1945 when the park was first established."[25]

The decade of the 1950s unfortunately did not produce the harmony for which Maxwell had optimistically hoped. The cougar population continued to grow to such serious proportions that the NPS even considered a policy of reducing the species. Park Service reports confirmed that ranchers and government trappers on properties adjacent to the park from 1952 through 1956 had killed over seventy-five mountain lions. In addition, in Big Bend itself a panther was disposed of after it seized a man's trouser leg along a popular hiking trail. Another cougar met a similar fate when a hunter tracked the animal into the park and a ranger dispatched it. Park Service employees by now assisted stockmen in their pursuit of predators, but rancher dissatisfaction with NPS wildlife policy continued.[26] Instead of rumors about the importation of wolves, a new one circulated about the Park Service bringing additional black bears into the park.[27] There was no validity to the allegations, but

---

24. Maxwell memorandum to Regional Director, Region III, February 10, 1949, File 204, BBNP, RG 79, NA; Director, Fish and Wildlife to Director, NPS, March 16, 1949, File 719, BBNP, RG 79, NA.

25. "Superintendent's Monthly Narrative Report, March, 1949," April 6, 1949, File 207-02.3, BBNP, RG 79, NA; San Angelo *Standard-Times*, March 13, 1949; Maxwell, "History of Big Bend National Park" (ms), 1952, BBNP Lib.

26. "Annual Animal Census Report for Big Bend National Park, 1951," BBNP Lib; "Biennial Animal Census Report for Big Bend National Park, 1952-1953," BBNP Lib; "Biennial Animal Census Report for Big Bend National Park, 1954-1955," BBNP Lib; O. C. Wallmo, "Work Study Report on Mountain Lions in Big Bend National Park, December 1952 to January, 1959," BBNP Lib.

27. Williams to Tom Connally, October 17, 1950, Records of Newton B. Drury, Director's Personal File: Big Bend National Park, 1940 to March, 1951,

the fact it was made indicated the existing hostility toward the NPS still held by some local ranchers. Further ill feelings occurred when one or more unidentified culprits spread poison throughout the park, which resulted in the death of more than twenty coyotes.[28]

The legal and occasional unlawful activities of a minority of stockmen, as well as climatic and ecological conditions, kept Big Bend's predator population stable throughout the 1960s. The number of cougars in the park has remained at an estimated strength of ten to twenty, while the golden eagle has become virtually extinct. Yet due to the nature of his business, the rancher must favor predatory control measures. He cannot fully accept or understand a policy that protects even the despised rattlesnake. But as long as no significant increase in Big Bend National Park's predators exists, charges that the park represents a "predator incubator" appear greatly exaggerated.[29]

RG 79, NA.

    28. "Annual Animal Census Report for Big Bend National Park, 1951," BBNP Lib.

    29. William O. Douglas, *Farewell to Texas: A Vanishing Wilderness* (New York: McGraw-Hill Book Company, 1967), pp. 159, 163; "Wildlife Inventory: Estimated Polulations of Certain Species in Areas of the National Park Service" (from 1963 to 1968 Field Reports), BBNP Lib.

VII Life on the Last Frontier

Big Bend's location in the largest and least accessible county in Texas contributed to the difficulties of its administration, protection, and visitor use.[1] In addition, problems after World War II arose because of the lack of funds for national parks. Other troubles concerned trespassing livestock as well as international border incidents, particularly smuggling activities, fear of hoof and mouth disease spreading from Mexico into the United States, and the proposed construction of a reservoir within the park boundaries.

In 1933 the state of Texas established Big Bend State Park with headquarters in the Chisos Basin and retained the responsibility of protecting the area until 1944. Since much of the land in the park was privately owned, protecting its natural resources proved difficult. Commercial curio dealers, for instance, removed truckloads of small, rare cacti from the park area for sale in souvenir shops. As long as these specimens came from private lands, the state was powerless to intervene.[2]

Wildlife was also threatened. Upon learning that the Colima

---

1. As noted in chapter four, the publicity campaign for the park constantly referred to Big Bend as America's "last frontier." A recent *National Geographic* article also echoed this theme as do the brochure issued by National Park Concessions, Inc. and an advertising flyer sent out by a real estate promoter. The latter encourages prospective buyers to purchase land soon before there is none left in "The Last of a Last Frontier." Nathaniel T. Kenney, "Big Bend: Jewel in the Texas Desert," *National Geographic*, CXXXIII (January, 1968), pp. 104–133. Ronnie C. Tyler, *The Big Bend: A History of the Last Texas Frontier* (Washington, D. C.: Department of the Interior/National Park Service, 1975) places it in its proper perspective, the Lone Star State's "last frontier."

2. A. F. Robinson to Secretary of the Interior, Conrad Wirth, and Herbert Maier, June 6, 1936, File 0–32, Part III, Big Bend National Park, Record Group 79, National Archives Building (hereafter cited as BBNP, RG 79, NA).

Warbler in the Chisos Range was near extinction, one individual tried to collect the skins of all the species possible for his private collection.[3] Fortunately he failed, but by the time the area had become a state park the gray wolf and bighorn sheep had already been destroyed or driven away. Among the endangered species that did survive were the peccary and the black bear. Meanwhile, the state enacted legislation in behalf of the threatened animals in the southern Brewster County section of the park. But there simply were not enough game wardens to enforce the measure adequately and the flora and fauna of the Big Bend would not be sufficiently protected until several years after the national park had become a reality. When it did open officially in July 1944, the small staff of five still were ineffective. But by the end of the decade the approximately fifty full and part-time workers were doing an adequate job of restoration and protection.[4]

The archaeology and paleontology of the Big Bend likewise suffered at the hands of vandals and souvenir collectors during the early years. When the Park Service unintentionally publicized information extolling the region's scientific wonders, institutions throughout the country hastened to the site to collect what they could before the federal government restricted their activities.[5] Even after the Park Service had issued warnings to the contrary, scientists from the American Museum of Natural History continued excavations. Today, hundreds of dinosaur bones, fossil shells, petrified wood, and other prehistoric specimens from the Big Bend area are displayed in museums throughout the country.[6]

---

3. William O. Douglas, *Farewell to Texas: A Vanishing Wilderness* (New York: McGraw-Hill Book Co., 1967), pp. 52–53.

4. George F. Baggley memorandum to Wirth, March 9, 1936, File O-32, Part III, BBNP, RG 79, NA; NPS Press Release, January 15, 1937, File O-32, Part IV, BBNP, RG 79, NA; Maier memorandum to Director, NPS, November 12, 1937, File O-32, Part IX, BBNP, RG 79, NA.

5. Arthur E. Demaray memorandum to Acting Regional Director, Region III, September 7, 1938, File O-32, Part VII, BBNP, RG 79, NA; Hillory Tolson to Clark Wissler, October 3, 1940, File O-32, Part VIII, BBNP, RG 79, NA.

6. It should be pointed out that executives of the American Museum of Natural History promised to comply with Park Service wishes. However, a few of their overzealous scientists for unknown reasons disregarded NPS requests. Roy Chapman Andrews to Tolson, October 11, 1940, File O-32, Part VIII, BBNP, RG

The success of Big Bend depended largely upon the selection of an able administrator. In 1943 Ross A. Maxwell, a tall, ruddy-faced Oklahoma farmboy, became the first superintendent, a position he would hold during the formative years of the park until 1952. He was well suited for the position, having received his doctorate in geology from Northwestern University in 1936, the same year that he began work in the Big Bend country as a young geologist.[7] In addition to having later produced several significant scientific publications,[8] Maxwell possessed the ability to get along with the local people. Indeed, he made many close friends while placating their anger over Park Service policies, especially in relation to predators and to grazing rights. One rancher remained an opponent of the Park Service throughout his life, yet he invariably exchanged Christmas cards with the Maxwell family and entertained them in his home.[9] An official of the Texas State Parks Board summed up the general feeling West Texans held for the superintendent: "Doc . . . is just as plain as an old shoe . . . the salt of the earth."[10]

Reflecting on his frontier experience at Big Bend years later,

---

79, NA; Demaray to Barnum Brown, July 31, 1940, File 0-32, Part VIII, BBNP, RG 79, NA; Demaray to Brown, September 5, 1940, File 0-32, Part VIII, BBNP, RG 79, NA; Kirk H. Scott to Brown, October 9, 1940, File 0-32, Part VIII, BBNP, RG 79, NA; Scott memorandum to Regional Director, Region III, October 10, 1940, File 0-32, Part VIII, BBNP, RG 79, NA; Fort Worth *Star-Telegram*, October 1, 1938; Ross A. Maxwell memorandum to W. F. Ayres, August 6, 1938, File 0-32, Part VII, BBNP, RG 79, NA.

7. Isabelle F. Story memorandum to Horton, October 19, 1943, File 201-10, BBNP, RG 79, NA; Dallas *Morning News* (clipping with no date), File 201-06, BBNP, RG 79, NA.

8. In addition to numerous articles, Maxwell has published two excellent books on Big Bend. See Ross A. Maxwell, John T. Lonsdale, Roy T. Hazzard, and John A. Wilson, *Geology of Big Bend National Park, Brewster County, Texas* (Austin: University of Texas, publication no. 6711, Bureau of Economic Geology, 1967); Maxwell, *The Big Bend of the Rio Grande: A Guide to the Rocks, Geologic History, and Settlers of the Area of Big Bend National Park* (Austin: University of Texas, Guidebook 7, Bureau of Economic Geology, 1968).

9. Maxwell memorandum to Regional Director, Region III, January 23, 1948, File 719, BBNP, RG 79, NA.

10. Frank Quinn to M. M. Harris, September 22, 1943, File 201-06, BBNP, RG 79, NA; M. R. Tillotson memorandum to Director, NPS, September 29, 1943, File 201-06, BBNP, RG 79, NA. After leaving the NPS Maxwell taught at the University of Texas until his retirement.

Maxwell observed: "The conditions were not as bad as [those] faced by the people who settled this area from 1840 to 1870. They had oxen and covered wagons—we had cars and trucks."[11] But that was about the only advantage. The nearest doctor was over eighty miles away and the closest public school was approximately the same distance. The park employees could do nothing about a physician, but they did do something about education. Parents tutored their own children until the fall of 1947 when the staff organized a public elementary school. Service employees subsequently voted thirteen to eight to raise the tax on each $100 valuation from ten to fifty cents so as to be eligible for state aid. One of the three school trustees was the chief park ranger, George Sholly, and another was Helen Maxwell, wife of the superintendent.[12] The same elementary school remains today, but older children attend high school in Alpine and return home each weekend. At the same time some employees prefer to obtain transfers when their children reach high school.[13]

Park wives also took the initiative in other areas and organized Sunday school classes and special Easter programs. Fifty-one people attended the first Easter service in 1949, including most of the local bachelors.[14] Various employees conducted church services for the adults on a rotating basis throughout the year. Several musicians on the staff got together infrequently for informal concerts, and later some of the children organized their own band.[15]

In general, Park Service personnel faced many hardships and deprivations during the 1940s. One of the greatest problems was ob-

---

11. Maxwell to the author, August 6, 1973.

12. Interview with Robert Wear, September 21, 1972; Maxwell memorandum to Regional Director, Region III, June 17, 1946, File 843–03, BBNP, RG 79, NA; "Superintendent's Monthly Narrative Report, August, 1947," September 4, 1947, File 207–02.3, BBNP, RG 79, NA; "Superintendent's Monthly Narrative Report, September, 1947," October 1, 1947, File 207–02.3, BBNP, RG 79, NA; "Superintendent's Monthly Narrative Report, April, 1948," May 6, 1948, File 207–02.3, BBNP, RG 79, NA.

13. William C. Everhart, *The National Park Service* (New York: Praeger Publishers, 1972), p. 159.

14. Maxwell memorandum to Regional Director, Region III, April 19, 1949, File 843–03, BBNP, RG 79, NA.

15. Interview with Robert Wear, September 21, 1972; Wear, "Where the Pavement Ends," *Texas Star*, May 21, 1972, p. 9.

taining fresh meat, milk, and eggs during the hot summer months. Maxwell asked permission of the regional and national offices of the Park Service for the staff to keep chickens and a cow, which normally was against Service regulations. The hierarchy argued that the Big Bend "pioneers" would have to get along primarily on canned foods.[16] A truck was sent to Marathon or Alpine once a month for supplies until 1949 when an Alpine grocery firm began making weekly deliveries. By then the seventeen families and several bachelors were consuming from $1,500 to $2,000 worth of food monthly, or more than enough to make deliveries profitable.[17]

Another hardship endured by the park personnel was the lack of communication with the outside world. Mail arrived only once a week at first, then increased to twice weekly. During the rainy season the unimproved Terlingua-Alpine road would sometimes be closed two weeks at a time. And even in the desert climate, snow could make the route impassable for as many as ten days out of the year.[18] By the 1970s mail deliveries into the Big Bend were being made regularly from Monday through Friday to the park headquarter's post office at Panther Junction.

Throughout the 1940s Big Bend National Park was eighty miles from the nearest telephone or telegraph station. In 1947 KULF, a local commercial radio station in Alpine, agreed to broadcast emergency messages to the park, but the arrangement would prove unsatisfactory for both parties. The following year another system was tried whereby the Border Patrol relayed messages to and from the park via short wave until 1953, when the Big Bend finally obtained telephone service.[19]

---

16. Maxwell memorandum to Regional Director, Region III, September 27, 1944, File 201-10, BBNP, RG 79, NA; Tolson memorandum to Regional Director, Region III, October 14, 1944, File 201-10, BBNP, RG 79, NA.

17. Maxwell to the author, August 6, 1973; Maxwell memorandum to Regional Director, Region III, February 11, 1949, File 900-05, BBNP, RG 79, NA; Tillotson memorandum to Superintendent, BBNP, February 15, 1949, File 900-05, BBNP, RG 79, NA.

18. Tolson to First Assistant Postmaster General, November 27, 1946, File 204, BBNP, RG 79, NA; Maxwell to H. K. Coale, June 27, 1947, File 204, BBNP, RG 79, NA; "Superintendent's Monthly Narrative Report, August, 1947," September 4, 1947, File 207-02.3, BBNP, RG 79, NA.

19. The park also has telegraph service. Maxwell memorandum to Director, NPS, July 21, 1944, File 660-04.3, BBNP, RG 79, NA; Tillotson to Glenn

Big Bend began its first year with an appropriation of only $15,000 for administrative purposes. Although the amount gradually increased,[20] the park remained understaffed and inadequately funded throughout the 1940s. Superintendent Ross Maxwell estimated that several national parks only a quarter the size of Big Bend had twice the number of rangers. Because of the isolated nature of the assignment, ranger positions and others were often unfilled for months. The men finally obtained were usually inexperienced and had to learn their jobs in the field. If fortunate, their living accommodations consisted of an abandoned shack without running water or sanitation facilities. As a rule, the employees worked overtime repairing broken well pumps, rounding up trespassing livestock, or doing other menial jobs. Not surprisingly, they sometimes suffered morale problems.[21] Maxwell occasionally combated "Big Bend fever" among his employees with a punch made of a "secret ingredient."[22]

One person who adapted very well to the rigorous life demanded by the Big Bend country was Maggie Smith, who operated the concession at Hot Springs on the Rio Grande. She has been called the "godmother to the Mexican people," a well deserved epithet. When a young Mexican couple came to her store with the woman in the advanced stages of labor, she loaded both in the back of her pickup truck and raced for the doctor in Marathon. They did not make it in time and Maggie had to deliver the baby by the side of the road. The mother and child fared well but the father was so overcome by the experience that he vomited during the entire trip back to Hot

---

Burgess, March 13, 1947, File 660–04.3, BBNP, RG 79, NA; Maxwell memorandum to Regional Director, Region III, March 6, 1948, File 660–04.3, BBNP, RG 79, NA.

20. The next year it was just over $25,000. The budget for fiscal year 1985 was $2,055,300. "Annual Report for BBNP," July 1, 1946, File 207, BBNP, RG 79, NA; *Hearings before a Subcommittee of the Committee on Appropriations, House of Representatives, 98th Cong., 2nd sess., Part I, Department of the Interior and Related Agencies Appropriations for 1985* (Washington, D. C.: Government Printing Office, 1984), p. 923.

21. Maxwell to Bernard DeVoto, November 22, 1948, File 504, BBNP, RG 79, NA; Maxwell memorandum to Director, NPS, May 28, 1947, File 204, BBNP, RG 79, NA; Maxwell's Advance Report, May 21, 1948, File 207, BBNP, RG 79, NA.

22. Interview with Robert Wear, September 21, 1972.

Springs.²³

Nevertheless, the Park Service hierarchy in Washington did not think too highly of Mrs. Smith. Concessions operators within the national parks were supposed to keep detailed, accurate records. Although a good "horsetrader," Maggie knew little about bookkeeping. "Mrs. Smith doesn't keep books," Superintendent Maxwell stated. "She sends in an order to the wholesaler at Alpine; the mail carrier delivers it to Hot Springs. She pays the bill and if there is any money left, that's profit. A Mexican comes from across the river and trades a goat skin for a sack of flour. The goat skin has a value, but can't be placed as an asset on anybody's books. If [it] is later sold for fifty cents, it goes into the little box and is used to pay for groceries the next week."²⁴ Since some sort of record had to be kept, park officials had no alternative but to accept whatever cash remained in the box at the end of the month.²⁵

A further indication of Big Bend's primitive nature were the place names of the region. Several topographical features of the park lacked any identification, while others possessed two or three. Many reflected the Spanish-Mexican heritage of the area and often the anglicized spelling had only a minor resemblance to the original Spanish. For example, *Mesa de Anquila* literally means Mesa of the Eels, a term hardly fitting its arid location.²⁶ All told, the United States Board of Geographical Names rendered approximately four dozen decisions for the Big Bend area.²⁷

---

23. Virginia Madison and Hallie Stillwell, *How Come It's Called That? Place Names in the Big Bend Country* (2nd ed.; New York: October House, Inc., 1968), pp. 49–50.

24. Maxwell memorandum to Regional Director, Region III, December 11, 1946, File 900, BBNP, RG 79, NA.

25. *Ibid.*

26. Other possibilities include Mesa of the Angels or Eagles since *anguila* could be the English corruption of the Spanish for angel (*angel*) or eagle (*aguila*). Both were more appropriate than Mesa of the Eels. Maxwell, *The Big Bend of the Rio Grande*, pp. 3–4.

27. The Board's decisions occasionally angered the local residents. For instance, Santa Helena became Santa Elena and Dead Horse Canyon was changed to Boquillas. Native Big Benders objected because several of the decisions such as the Dead Horse Canyon example erased names very much a part of the folkore and legends of the region. Maxwell memorandum to Superintendent Edmund Rogers, Yellowstone NP, May 20, 1946, File 731-01, BBNP, RG 79, NA; *Decisions of the*

More than 150,000 tourists visited Big Bend on the edge of the American frontier during the decade of the 1940s. Since the concessioners did not handle perishable items, the tourists had to bring most of their food supplies from the outside. Gasoline was available in the park toward the end of the decade, but it sold for five cents above the price charged at Alpine. None of the park's one hundred miles of primary roads were paved. Moreover, the heaviest visitation came during the rainy season between June and September. Although the average for these months was slightly more than an inch and one-half, most of this fell within the space of an hour or two. Thus, park visitors frequently found themselves trapped by flashfloods which swept down one or several of the fifty arroyos that criscrossed the principal roads. Measuring sticks at the crossings indicated when the waters had subsided enough for fording. There were only three culverts in the entire park. Overnight facilities consisted of a few one-room, tar paper huts left over from CCC days. Before Big Bend obtained electrical service in 1953, these shelters had to depend upon kerosene or gasoline lanterns for light. There also were several primitive campsites at Santa Elena Canyon and the Chisos Basin.[28]

In 1956 the Park Service initiated Mission 66, a long range conservation and improvement project. The ten year program was so named because most of the master plan was to be completed by 1966, the fiftieth anniversary of the National Park Service. Over one billion dollars would be spent in the national parks developing the physical facilities and providing trained personnel for interpretive and protective programs.[29] Big Bend profited by the pavement of approximately one hundred miles of road and the construction of bridges over the more troublesome arroyos. A headquarters building at Panther Junction and a new modern lodge complex were constructed in the Basin with accommodations for over 200 guests. In addition, several hundred trailer and camp sites were built in the

---

United States Board of Geographical Names: Decisions Rendered Between July 1, 1938 and June 30, 1939 (Washington, D. C.: Government Printing Office, 1939).

28. Maxwell to DeVoto, November 22, 1948, File 504, BBNP, RG 79, NA; Tolson memorandum to Director, NPS, and Regional Offices, July 15, 1944, File 601, Part II, BBNP, RG 79, NA; Herold Radcliff memorandum to Regional Forester, Region III, November 24, 1948, BBNP, RG 79, NA.

29. Everhart, *The National Park Service*, pp. 34-37.

Basin and on the Rio Grande with sufficient drinking water and conveniently located flush toilets. By 1966 there were four grocery stores within the park area, but because of high prices visitors generally brought in their supplies from adjoining towns, just as they did in the 1940s.[30]

Modern conveniences and improvements throughout the rugged area today belie its tradition of violence. In 1900, the explorer Robert T. Hill called it the "Bloody Bend," because the region seemed to attract the worst elements from both sides of the border. One of the most famous local incidents, a raid by Mexican bandits upon Glenn Springs, occurred in May 1916. Three soldiers of the Fourteenth Infantry, United States Army were killed, as well as several civilians and an undetermined number of Mexicans. Although conditions are much more peaceful today, bullet-ridden bodies occasionally are found floating in the shallow waters of the Rio Grande.[31]

Mexican nationals who processed and smuggled candelilla wax out of the park formerly caused considerable worry to the staff. The undermanned Park Service simply could not stop the practice, but more or less managed to keep it under control. On December 6, 1948 two park rangers sighted a party of fifty to seventy-five Mexicans near Santa Elena Canyon with thirteen processing vats and approximately one hundred mules and donkeys. The rangers later captured three of the culprits, as well as several donkeys and a substantial amount of wax. One of those arrested was a tearful fourteen year old boy whom the rangers later released on his promise that he would never cross the border illegally again. The two men were then taken to court and sentenced to ninety days in jail. News of the arrest and subsequent conviction put an immediate but temporary stop to the activities near Santa Elena Canyon. Because it is there for the taking and brings a good price, wax processing and smuggling have continued

---

30. More detailed information on the park facilities can be obtained from a general information bulletin from the Superintendent, BBNP. The author noted a disparity, for instance, in the price of beer, a necessity for some after a hot day hiking in the desert. In August 1972 premium brands purchased outside of BBNP cost $1.35 per six pack. Park concessions sold the same for $2.00.

31. Robert T. Hill, "Running the Cañons of the Rio Grande: A Chapter of Recent Exploration," *Century Magazine*, LXI (January, 1901), p. 371; O. L. Shipman, *Taming of the Big Bend* (Marfa, Texas: privately published, 1926), p. 148; Madison and Stillwell, *How Come It's Called That?*, p. 42; Interview with Ronnie C. Tyler, October 10, 1973.

at Big Bend, but regular patrols and occasional convictions have kept it minimal.[32]

Mexican livestock which crossed the Rio Grande constituted another international problem for park personnel. It first merely taxed the already overgrazed vegetation of the Big Bend, but matters became more serious when an epidemic of hoof and mouth disease broke out in 1947. Obviously the small staff could not patrol a hundred miles of the international border adequately and maintain an effective quarantine. Accordingly, the Bureau of Animal Industry in the United States Department of Agriculture employed special River Riders, varying in number from nine to thirty-five. In addition, employees of the Texas Livestock Sanitation Commission sometimes assisted in patrol work. At first these special details were under orders to confine their activities to turning the strays back across the river. Later, officials in Washington authorized the destruction of all Mexican livestock found in the United States except horses, donkeys, burros, and mules. The latter did not carry the disease, but nevertheless were subject to impoundment. Their owners subsequently had to pay substantial fines before recovering the property.[33]

On one occasion authorities seized eighty-seven horses and informed the owners that it would cost them eighteen dollars for each animal. The angry Mexicans claimed only one of their horses legally, then a few nights later they successfully rustled fifty-eight more. Needless to say, events such as this did little to insure good relations between the people on both sides of the border. Among other disagreeable activities was the poaching of deer in the park and the dynamiting of fish in the Rio Grande on the part of Mexican nationals.[34]

---

32. Sholly memorandum to Superintendent, BBNP, December 8, 1948, File 208-48, BBNP, RG 79, NA; "Superintendent's Monthly Narrative Report, December, 1948," January 7, 1949, File 207-02.3, BBNP, RG 79, NA; "Superintendent's Monthly Narrative Report, January, 1949," February 7, 1949, File 207-02.3, BBNP, RG 79, NA.

33. "Superintendent's Monthly Narrative Report, Feb. 1948," March 8, 1948, File 207-02.3, BBNP, RG 79, NA; Maxwell memorandum to Regional Director, Region III, Feb. 28, 1947, File 208-48, BBNP, RG 79, NA; "Superintendent's Monthly Narrative Report, April, 1947," May 9, 1947, File 207-02.3, BBNP, RG 79, NA; Maxwell memorandum to Regional Director, Region III, August 3, 1948, File 208-48, BBNP, RG 79, NA.

34. Jose Pontones to Superintendent, BBNP, April 21, 1949, File 208-06,

Incidents along the border have continued to the present. The park still does not have enough manpower to keep out Mexican livestock which cross over from Coahuila and Chihuahua. Fortunately, there is no longer any danger of hoof and mouth disease. However, employees have the larger problems today in protecting camps along the river from looters, patrolling the border for "wetbacks," and in combating the flow of marijuana, heroin, cocaine, and other drugs from Mexico. On one occasion in 1972, Ranger George Howarth intercepted a well known smuggler known as "Bronco." When the ranger drew his gun, "Bronco" did likewise. The two men stared at one another until the smuggler retraced his footsteps back across the shallow river. "It's probably a good thing George didn't try to stop him," Superintendent Joe Carithers later remarked. "Somebody would've gotten hurt."[35]

Another hazard encountered by the rangers is that of grass and forest fires, which are particularly dangerous during drought. Lightning has caused many fires and extensive damage to plant life, especially in the Chisos Mountains area. Fire fanned by brisk winds can spread rapidly through the tall and highly volatile basket grass and destroy thousands of acres of flora and fauna that make Big Bend a unique land of contrasts. During the CCC period, a conflagration of undetermined origin destroyed the museum in the Basin and hundreds of specimens collected by Maxwell and others. Toward the end of the 1940s increased appropriations, a larger staff, war surplus fire fighting equipment, and an improved water supply minimized considerably the dangers from fires.[36]

For several summers after the park opened, white-tail deer in the region mysteriously died by the hundred. The symptoms differed

---

BBNP, RG 79, NA; Maxwell to Pontones, April 27, 1949, File 208–06, BBNP, RG 79, NA; "Superintendent's Monthly Narrative Report, February, 1949," March 9, 1949, File 207–02.3, BBNP, RG 79, NA.

    35. Jack Hope, "Big Bend: A Nice Place to Visit," *Audubon*, LXXV (July, 1973), p. 46.

    36. Loyd Wade to Frank Quinn, May 24, 1944, File 883–01, Part I, BBNP, RG 79, NA; P. P. Patraw telegram to Director, NPS, April 21, 1948, File 883–03.1, BBNP, RG 79, NA; "Statement of Elmer Davenport, Project Superintendent, Museum Fire of December 26, 1941," December 29, 1941, File 883–05, Part I, BBNP, RG 79, NA. Reading through the Superintendent's Monthly Narrative Reports from 1944 through 1949 indicates the difficulty of preventing and controlling fires and the progress made.

slightly from one season to the next and the staff was uncertain whether the animals suffered from malnutrition and unusually dry weather or from organic infections. Interestingly enough, no other fauna in the area was affected, including the black-tail, or mule deer. Since the park had no veterinarian, the dead animals were rushed to the state agricultural experimental station at Sonora, more than two hundred miles eastward. Even with the carcasses iced down, none made it to the station before putrefacation had set in, thus making it quite difficult to learn much from the autopsy. When the drought finally ended, the malady abated dramatically.[37]

Another species of "wildlife" which caused the rangers much concern was the burro. These hearty animals numbered from 500 to 1,000 and not only constituted a serious threat to the vegetation but also cut hundreds of miles of paths throughout the park. The employees at first simply rounded the burros up and auctioned them off. But the procedure proved too costly and time consuming and the rangers finally resorted to shooting them and leaving the carcasses for scavengers. The same practice was also carried out on the feral goats until their numbers were reduced to the point that they no longer are a threat to the natural environment.[38]

One of the greatest domestic difficulties during the 1940s was caused by livestock which wandered into the park from neighboring ranches to deplete the vegetation. In addition, some ranchers who moved from the area when it became a park purposely abandoned their livestock.[39] Superintendent Maxwell and local ranchers tried to

---

37. Matt N. Dodge memorandum to Superintendent, BBNP, July 21, 1945, File 715–04, BBNP, RG 79, NA; F. M. Shigley, "Report on White-tail Deer Deaths," September 4, 1948, File 715–04, BBNP, RG 79, NA; Sholly memorandum to Superintendent, BBNP, September 8, 1948, File 715–04, BBNP, RG 79, NA; W. T. Hardy to to E. G. Marsh, Jr., September 8, 1948, File 715–04, BBNP, RG 79, NA; Maxwell memorandum to Regional Director, Region III, October 14, 1948, File 715–04, BBNP, RG 79, NA; Victor H. Cahalane memorandum to Chief, Division of Wildlife Research, Fish and Wildlife Service, October 26, 1948, File 715–04, BBNP, RG 79, NA.

38. Ratcliff memorandum to Regional Forester, Region III, November 24, 1948, File 715, BBNP, RG 79, NA; Maxwell memorandum to Regional Director, Region III, December 27, 1948, File 715, BBNP, RG 79, NA; Director, NPS memorandum to Regional Director, Region III, January 27, 1949, File 715, BBNP, RG 79, NA.

39. Newton B. Drury to Ken Regan, May 11, 1949, File 204, BBNP, RG 79, NA; "Superintendent's Monthly Narrative Report, May 1947," June 6,

get Congress to appropriate money to fence in the park area, but to no avail. Texas law did require property owners to fence in their acres if they wished to keep trespassing stock off their land. Neighboring ranchers thought the statute applied to Big Bend National Park, which would have meant that the Service must build a fence around the park. However, there already were federal statutes on the books which charged adjacent property owners with the responsibility of keeping their animals off of government lands.[40]

Because of misunderstandings which arose over the various legal technicalities, ill-feelings developed when rangers seized stray stock and charged the owners as much as eighteen dollars each for returning them. "I cannot understand why it should be legal for a federal bureau to do something that in the case of an individual would be prosecuted as horse theft," one rancher wrote to his congressman.[41] Nevertheless, Big Bend's livestock population had been reduced by the end of the 1940s from 40,000 head to only a few hundred on the privately owned lands. By this time, trespassing stock occupied less and less of the rangers's time.[42] Today, most of the neighboring ranches are enclosed with fences and the little trespassing that does exist usually is caused by stray animals from Mexico.

At various times, dam builders have threatened national park sites at Yosemite, Kings Canyon, Grand Canyon, Dinosaur National Monument, and Big Bend. The latter location was particularly appealing because it lay on the Mexican-United States boundary and possessed three deep, narrow canyons. The construction of a series of reservoirs was one means of developing friendly relations between

---

1947, File 207-02.3, BBNP, RG 79, NA; Maxwell's Advance Report, May 21, 1948, File 207, BBNP, RG 79, NA; "Superintendent's Monthly Narrative Report, November, 1947," December 5, 1947, File 207-02.3, BBNP, RG 79, NA.

40. Drury to Regan, May 11, 1949, File 204, BBNP, RG 79, NA; Maxwell memorandum to Regional Director, Region III, October 29, 1947, File 208-48, BBNP, RG 79, NA; John M. Davis to John A. Grambling, February 25, 1949, File 208-48, BBNP, RG 79, NA.

41. H. W. Patterson to Regan, April 18, 1949, File 208-48, BBNP, RG 79, NA.

42. However, trespass grazing was still an expensive problem. For instance, the least illegal grazing since the park opened occurred during 1948. Yet over $4,500 was spent to remove 423 head of trespassing stock. Maxwell's Advance Report, May 21, 1948, File 207, BBNP, RG 79, NA; "1945 Annual Report, BBNP," July 6, 1945, File 207, BBNP, RG 79, NA.

provided that the International Boundary Commission must keep the Park Service apprised of any possible dam development in the park. Nevertheless, if one of Big Bend's canyons were chosen, the Service had no recourse but to accept the decision.[47]

Throughout the latter 1940s investigations proceeded in the park with Boquillas and Mariscal Canyons receiving strong consideration. The Park Service could only hope that the development already taking place in Big Bend would deter any dam construction in or near the park. Eventually the International Boundary Commission rejected the sites in Big Bend mainly because of its isolation from markets for electrical power and the absence of sufficient irrigable land. Subsequent construction of Falcon and Amistad Reservoirs south of the park apparently have ended the possibility of a dam in or near Big Bend National Park.[48]

In the late 20th century the Big Bend country and park still remain largely undeveloped, uncivilized, and sparsely settled. Except for an occasional act of violence, employees frequently suffer from isolation and boredom during winter months. Some compare assignment to the Big Bend as equivalent to military service and literally "count the days" until their tour of duty will terminate. At the same time, park families now enjoy television and air conditioned houses and most enjoy living and working in the "last frontier." As Ross Maxwell remarked in a letter to this writer regarding his years in the Big Bend, "My wife and I are too old to pioneer another new park development, but neither of us would have missed our pleasant

---

not apply to Big Bend. The treaty abrogated this provision. Treaty Series 994 "Utilization of Waters of the Colorado and Tijuana Rivers and of the Rio Grande: Treaty Between the United States of America and Mexico," signed at Washington, D. C. February 3, 1944; ratified by Mexico October 16, 1945; effective November 8, 1949 (transcript of the treaty in File 660–05.4, BBNP, RG 79, NA).

47. "Memorandum of Understanding as to Functions and Jurisdiction of Agencies of the United States in Relation to the Colorado and Tijuana Rivers and the Rio Grande below Fort Quitman, Texas under Water Treaty signed at Washington, February 3, 1944," File 660–05.4, BBNP, RG 79, NA; Jackson Price memorandum to Wirth, November 24, 1948, File 660–05.4, BBNP, RG 79, NA; Tillotson memorandum to Superintendent, BBNP, December 21, 1948, File 660–05.4, BBNP, RG 79, NA.

48. Tillotson memorandum to Director, NPS, May 25, 1944, File 660–05.4, BBNP, RG 79, NA; L. M. Lawson to Tillotson, September 14, 1948, File 660–05.4, BBNP, RG 79, NA; Tillotson memorandum to Director, NPS, February 17, 1949, File 660–05.4, BBNP, RG 79, NA.

memories and experiences."[49]

---

49. Maxwell to the author, August 6, 1973.

VIII National or International Park?

A principal objective of President Franklin D. Roosevelt was the realization of a "Good Neighbor" foreign policy with other countries of the western hemisphere. One way to achieve such a goal, especially with Mexico and Canada, would be to create international parks, monuments, and wildlife and forest reserves along our northern and southern boundaries. As early as 1932 the Waterton-Glacier International Peace Park had been established in Montana and the Canadian province of Alberta.[1] The National Park Service later proposed similar projects with Mexico, including the Organ Pipe Cactus Monument in Arizona and Sonora, Coronado Memorial in New Mexico and Chihuahua, and Big Bend International Park in Texas, Chihuahua, and Coahuila.

The Alpine, Texas Chamber of Commerce in 1933 proposed locating a "Friendly Nations" park on the United States-Mexican border. Its director hired a local landscape architect to prepare appropriate plans. A. W. Dorgan subsequently produced several elaborate studies, which would have created a vast world's fair complex on the present site of Big Bend National Park. Among other things, he envisioned a series of dams for electric power, irrigation, and recreation, and a "Highway Americana," which would pass through the park and connect Alaska with Argentina. The Big Bend area would offer excellent hotels and a theater where orchestras from each of the twenty-one countries in the western hemisphere would perform

---

1. Rotarians suggested the idea for the United States-Canadian international park. Both the United States and Canadian parks had "existed previously and each continued under its own national administration." Hillory Tolson to Richard Kendrick, January 13, 1945, File 504, Big Bend National Park, Record Group 79, National Archives Building (hereafter cited as BBNP, RG 79, NA).

from time to time. Dorgan's proposals also called for countries of the western hemisphere to exhibit their folklore, art, costumes, and other aspects of native life. Big Bend could become a "living example of World Peace" and international cooperation.[2]

Others also saw the international potential of the Big Bend, although not in the grandiose manner of Dorgan. In January 1935, E. E. Townsend of Alpine recommended to the Park Service that Mexico create a sister park adjacent to the proposed Big Bend National Park. Townsend believed the project would foster friendship between two peoples "now almost unknown to each other."[3] At the same time, D. E. Colp, head of the Texas State Parks Board, informed the Park Service of his agency's desire for an international park on the Rio Grande. He tried unsuccessfully to arrange a flight over the proposed area in Texas, Chihuahua, and Coahuila by the governors of these states to acquaint them with the scenic grandeur of the region.[4]

Several weeks later United States Senator Morris Sheppard took the first official action toward the creation of the park when he suggested the idea to President Roosevelt.[5] As we have seen, the President's enthusiasm for the project helped speed the Big Bend legislation through Congress in a record sixty-three days. Forty-eight hours after the Big Bend legislation became law, Secretary of the Interior Harold Ickes asked Secretary of State Cordell Hull to contact Mexican officials and solicit their support for the international park

---

2. A. W. Dorgan to Harold Ickes, October 8, 1934, File 0–32, Part I, BBNP, RG 79, NA; Dorgan to Morris Sheppard and Tom Connally, August 28, 1935, File 0–32, Part I, BBNP, RG 79, NA. Dorgan persistently supported his scheme through the years. See Dorgan to Cordell Hull, May 12, 1940, File 0–32, Part VIII, BBNP, RG 79, NA; [BHT] Ben H. Thompson to Mrs. Benson, July 31, 1942, File 0–32, Part IX, BBNP, RG 79, NA. In 1945 Horace Morelock, president of Sul Ross State Teachers College in Alpine, submitted a plan in many ways identical with Dorgan's. See Morelock's manuscript, "The Acropolis of the Americas," File 501, BBNP, RG 79, NA; Dallas *Morning News*, January 22, 1945.

3. "Report of the Big Bend Area, Texas," January, 1935, File 207, BBNP, RG 79, NA.

4. Colp to Sam Rayburn, January 17, 1935, Box A–1, Bastrop State Park Warehouse, Bastrop, Texas (hereafter cited as Bastrop SPW); Josephus Daniels to Rayburn, January 31, 1935, Box A–1, Bastrop SPW.

5. Sheppard to Roosevelt, February 16, 1935, File 0–32, Part I, BBNP, RG 79, NA.

proposal which "seems to mean so much in the way of good will and mutual understanding between these two neighboring countries."[6]

Mexico already had made plans for a forest reserve and game sanctuary in the northeastern section of the state of Chihuahua opposite the proposed Big Bend park.[7] American diplomatic and Park Service officials hoped that she would go further and designate the area as a national park. In August 1935, Josephus Daniels, the American ambassador, talked with Miguel A. de Quevedo, head of Mexico's Department of Forestry, Fish, and Game[8] and found him "most enthusiastic" about the proposed international park. Quevedo even suggested that representatives from both countries meet as soon as possible to discuss the matter.[9]

In the fall of 1935 two conferences regarding the international project were held in El Paso. The chief negotiators were Herbert Maier of the United States Park Service and Quevedo and Daniel Galicia, an engineer in the Mexican Forestry, Fish, and Game Department. The talks quickly revealed that the Mexican representatives had not yet investigated the Big Bend area and were unfamiliar with United States Park Service policies which called for the preservation of the environment in its natural condition. Maier learned, for instance, that Quevedo's main interests were resource exploitation and reforestation programs rather than scenic preservation. For example, Theodore Roosevelt had once invited Quevedo to Washington while Gifford Pinchot was head of the United States Forest Service. The Mexican bureaucrat had subsequently become an ardent disciple of Pinchot's resource utilization programs, which consistently clashed with Park Service policies.[10]

---

6. Ickes to Secretary of State, June 22, 1935, File 0-32, Part I, BBNP, RG 79, NA.

7. Daniels to Secretary of State, July 27, 1935, File 0-32, Part I, BBNP, RG 79, NA.

8. This agency had jurisdiction over Mexico's national parks and was part of the Deparment of Agriculture.

9. Daniels to Secretary of State, August 16, 1935, File 0-32, Part I, BBNP, RG 79, NA; Quevedo to Daniels, September 20, 1935, File 0-32, Part II, BBNP, RG 79, NA.

10. "Report on Conference with Mexican Representatives in Connection with Proposed Big Bend National Park," October 5, 1935, Big Bend National Park Library (hereafter cited as BBNP Lib); "Report on Conference with Mexican

Yet even with these differences and misunderstandings, the conferences proved beneficial after each side had expressed enthusiasm over the possibility of a series of international projects along the Mexican-United States border. The two parties agreed that Mexico would eventually establish its own park contiguous to Big Bend. Each would be under the administration of its respective country, with citizens from Mexico and the United States enjoying unrestricted access. Before the second conference adjourned, a joint commission was appointed to investigate the international park idea, recommend boundaries, and keep Mexican and United States officials apprised of future progress.[11]

In February 1936, the commission examined the proposed park site and specifically studied international and wildlife issues.[12] Later studies by Mexican and American specialists revealed that the Mexican scenery was equal if not superior to that on the American side.[13] The fauna was more abundant and the grass lands had not been overgrazed to the extent of those in Texas.[14] Protection afforded by park status for the Mexican and United States lands would insure an ecological balance.[15] Also, the Mexican lands provided a model by which to measure the recovery of the flora and fauna of the Big Bend from the abuses of overgrazing.[16]

Representatives Relative to the Proposed Big Bend International Park and Other Border Areas," November 24, 1935, File 0-32, Part II, BBNP, RG 79, NA.

11. *Ibid.*; El Paso *Times*, November 25, 1935.

12. Dallas *Morning News*, February 16, 1936; El Paso *Times*, February 16, 1936; NPS Press Release, February 16, 1936, File 0-32, Part III, BBNP, RG 79, NA; Carroll H. Wegemann, "Diary of a Trip from Alpine, Texas to the Big Bend and Old Mexico with the International Park Commission," February 17, 1936, File 204, BBNP, RG 79, NA.

13. Alpine *Avalanche*, September 18, 1936; Tolson to Kendrick, January 13, 1944, File 504, BBNP, RG 79, NA; Department of the Interior Press Release, November 8, 1936, File 0-32, Part III, BBNP, RG 79, NA; Victor H. Cahalane to Conrad Wirth, October 13, 1944, File 718, BBNP, RG 79, NA.

14. C. C. Presnall, "Field Notes on the Big Bend National Park and Mexico, March 31-April 17, 1945," April 25, 1945, File 204, BBNP, RG 79, NA.

15. Walter P. Taylor, Walter B. McDougall, and William B. Davis, "Preliminary Report of an Ecological Survey of Big Bend National Park, March-June, 1944," File 204, BBNP, RG 79, NA.

16. Ernest Marsh, Jr., "Biological Survey of the Santa Rosa and Del Carmen Mountains of Northern Coahuila, Mexico, July 2-September 22, 1936,"

The United States and Mexico seemed intent on achieving as quickly as possible the goal of an international park. Mexico requested Arno B. Cammerer, Director of the Park Service, and two other Service men, Roger Toll and George Wright, both of whom belonged to the international commission, to make an additional inspection of the Mexican side. The trip never materialized for Toll and Wright were killed in an automobile accident a short time later. Until their positions on the commission could be filled, formal discussions with Mexico did not resume until fall, 1936.[17]

The new joint commission met in El Paso in November of that year and approved common eastern and western boundaries of the international park. Other points discussed included a vehicle bridge, free visitor access to both sides, and the United States Bureau of Reclamation's tentative decision not to place dams inside the proposed boundaries. Cammerer agreed with the Mexican representatives that no road should be built along the Rio Grande since it would obstruct the flow of wildlife across the river.[18]

Prior to the meeting, Daniel Galicia had pointed out to the United States Park Service that the Mexican Forestry Department was considerably lacking in qualified personnel. Moreover, the idea of national parks had not yet gained widespread acceptance in Mexico. A severely restricted budget had kept her from acquiring the 400–500,000 acres required for her portion of the international park.[19] The Park Service was well aware of the situation and would try various measures to promote the national park concept in Mexico. Over the next decade Service officials invited Mexican leaders to tour some of America's more prominent national parks at United States's expense.[20] At the same time, Park Service employees and private in-

---

March 10, 1937, File 204, BBNP, RG 79, NA.

17. Alpine *Avalanche*, September 3, 1948; Director, NPS memorandum to Ickes, February 29, 1936, File 0-32, Part III, BBNP, RG 79, NA; Wirth to Regional Officer, Region III, June 29, 1936, File 0-32, Part III, BBNP, RG 79, NA.

18. Maier to Director, NPS, November 13, 1936, File 0-32, Part III, BBNP, RG 79, NA.

19. Galicia to Maier, September 23, 1936, File 0-32, Part III, BBNP, RG 79, NA.

20. Maier to Wirth, July 3, 1936, File 0-32, Part IV, BBNP, RG 79, NA; M. R. Tillotson memorandum to Director, NPS, December 14, 1945, Records of

dividuals made numerous trips to Mexico City, Chihuahua, Saltillo, and elsewhere to promote an international park. They distributed brochures explaining United States national park principles, spoke on radio programs, and talked with chambers of commerce directors and other civic organizations.[21] However, the campaign failed to produce authorization for the proposed Mexican national park opposite Big Bend, Sierra del Carmens.

Perhaps a major reason for the Mexican government's attitude toward Sierra del Carmen was the nine year delay by the state of Texas in purchasing the Big Bend lands. At the first international conference in October 1935 and subsequent discussions, Mexican officials indicated they would take appropriate action as soon as Texas deeded its acres to the federal government.[22] This finally occurred in 1944 when the United States and Mexico were in the midst of World War II.

In September 1944, Newton B. Drury, Cammerer's successor as Director of the Park Service, suggested to Roosevelt that he write the Mexican president, Avila Camacho, and express the hope that the Mexican park would become a reality soon after the war ended.[23] Camacho replied that he agreed fully with Roosevelt's wishes and that he had already instructed the appropriate departments to begin studies for the creation of a Mexican national park adjacent to Big

---

the National Park Service, Central Classified Files, 1907–1949, File 0–32, Big Bend Proposed International Park, Part I, RG 79, NA (hereafter cited as NPS Files, BBIP, RG 79, NA).

21. L. A. Garrison, "A History of the Proposed Big Bend International Park," July 6, 1953 (revised April 1, 1954), BBNP Lib; "Partial Text of Radio Speech Broadcast Over Mexican Station XEFI, Chihuahua City, Chihuahua, 6:00 P.M., June 18, 1945," File 207, BBNP, RG 79, NA; Tillotson to Ricardo Villareal, March 13, 1945, File 501, BBNP, RG 79, NA; Tillotson memorandum to Director, NPS, June 30, 1945, File 207, BBNP, RG 79, NA.

22. "Report on Conference with Mexican Representatives in Connection with Proposed Big Bend National Park," October 5, 1935, BBNP Lib; Newton B. Drury telegram to Associate Director, NPS, September 7, 1943, File 601, Part II, BBNP, RG 79, NA; Department of the Interior Press Release, July 21, 1941, File 501, BBNP, RG 79, NA.

23. Drury memorandum to Secretary of the Interior, September 16, 1944, File 601, Part II, BBNP, RG 79, NA; Roosevelt to Manuel Avila Camacho, October 24, 1944, Records of Newton B. Drury, Director's Personal File, Big Bend National Park, 1940 to March, 1951, RG 79, NA (hereafter cited as Drury File, BBNP, RG 79, NA).

Bend.[24]

World War II ended in August 1945 and despairing critics now realized that Mexico still did not understand the fundamental concepts of the United States national park policy, an important prerequisite to the realization of the international project. Minor R. Tillotson, Southwest regional director, and Ross A. Maxwell, superintendent of Big Bend, visited Cumbres de Majalca National Park in Chihuahua and found that Mexican policies differed substantially from those of the United States Park Service. For example, lumbering was prohibited, but Mexican citizens could gather dead wood. Entrepreneurs therefore would girdle trees in the park and harvest them the following season. Later, the Mexican government granted concessions for the outright cutting of timber within her national parks. In addition, individuals could purchase land inside the parks for private homes or commercial ventures. Since there were no building restrictions, dilapidated shacks existed by the side of expensive Spanish-style dwellings. Tillotson and Maxwell likewise discovered that an artificial lake was planned to provide recreation for park visitors, another policy contradictory to those of the United States Park Service.[25] Apparently, Mexico's conception of national parks remained what it had been when negotiations for the international project first began in 1935.

In spite of this, some Mexican officials expressed enthusiasm for the idea, but most were not in positions of real power or influence to accomplish anything. Various secretaries of agriculture, who had ultimate jurisdiction over the country's national preserves, took little or no interest in the park. The same held true for the governors of Chihuahua and Coahuila.[26] But one of the chief reasons for the stalemate regarding the international project was Mexico's

---

24. Camacho to Roosevelt, November 30, 1944, Drury File, BBNP, RG 79, NA.

25. Tillotson memorandum to Director, NPS, June 30, 1945, File 207, BBNP, RG 79, NA; Tillotson memorandum to Director, NPS, December 14, 1945, NPS Files, BBIP, RG 79, NA; William Vogt to Cahalane, March 25, 1945, NPS Files, BBIP, RG 79, NA.

26. Maurice Minchen to Mae M. Ament, March 18, 1945, File 501, BBNP, RG 79, NA; Wirth to Glenn Burgess, October 5, 1944, File 601, Part II, BBNP, RG 79, NA; Tillotson memorandum to Director, NPS, September 25, 1944, File 719, BBNP, RG 79, NA.

deep-rooted animosities toward the "Colossus to the North."

In November 1945 William Vogt, chief of the conservation section of the Pan American Union, obtained two confidential Mexican reports on the international park and forwarded them to Director Drury and to the State Department. Vogt observed that the documents indicated "a complete lack of understanding of the Big Bend situation and considerable opposition to going ahead with the park."[27] One of the documents noted that Big Bend possessed attractions for the tourist, but its remoteness made it among "the least frequented" of the American national parks. Moreover, the United States evidently had declared it a national park because she could find no better use for the land. The same report stated that the proposed park area in northern Coahuila had greater economic potential if used for other purposes. Although growth was slow in the Sierra del Carmens because of climatic conditions, the region did have a density of trees which yielded an excellent lumber crop. The best wooded section, incidentally, was owned by an American corporation.[28]

The second confidential report revealed that Mexican lands also were capable of supporting a substantial cattle industry. For example, retired Mexican army general Miguel L. Gonzales owned a large cattle operation in northern Coahuila and successfully utilized conservational ranching methods. If the park were created, he obviously would lose his land. Not surprisingly, he opposed the idea vehemently and warned the Director of the Forestry Department of the danger of setting aside a large portion of land for a park. He further reminded the official that the United States had previously violated agreements with Mexico, and, that if a large border area were set aside, "the Mexican people will benefit in no way whatsoever."[29]

---

27. Vogt to Drury, November 6, 1945, Drury File, BBNP, RG 79, NA. Vogt later wrote the classic study of the Hispanic world view concerning the environment. See his *Road to Survival* (New York: William Sloane Associates, Inc., 1948). Chapter seven deals with the origin and perpetuation of anti-environmentalism in Latin American countries.

28. "Report of the Study Made in La Sierra del Carmen, Coahuila, for the Creation of an International Park between the United States and Mexico," Drury File, BBNP, RG 79, NA.

29. Memorandum to Director General, Directoral General of Forestry and Hunting, June 12, 1945, Drury File, BBNP, RG 79, NA.

Because of the tremendous expenses that would be involved in the development and maintenance of an isolated desert park, the first report concluded that the project would cause more strife than "good neighborliness." Finally, if Sierra del Carmens were established as a park, exploitation of the forest and cattle resources should continue because "it would not be advisable . . . to segregate something that contributes to the strengthening of the [Mexican] national economy."[30]

Surprisingly, Mexican economic arguments against a national park received support from Clifford C. Presnall of the United States Fish and Wildlife Service. He had previously inspected the region on both sides of the Rio Grande, including the Gonzales ranch, and regarded Mexican national park policies as a sham. Presnall quickly become convinced that conservative cattle ranching would be the best use of the land.[31] Presnall's statement, plus the adverse reports of the Mexican Forestry and Hunting Department and the evidence of abuse of her already existing national parks, supported the idea that Mexico was primarily responsible for the failure to implement the international park. According to some Americans, the Latins would only proceed with the project if the United States would pay most of the development and administrative costs.[32] Such criticism was well founded because Mexican officials believed that only American tourists would benefit from the international park. Moreover, their numbers would be so small that the occasional visitor to the Mexican portion would not add significantly to Mexico's revenues from tourism.[33]

Soon after he became president, Harry S. Truman urged Camacho to issue a proclamation in behalf of the proposed international park. United States Park Service officials met in Mexico City in

---

30. "Report on the Study Made in La Sierra del Carmen, Coahuila, for the Creation of an International Park between the United States and Mexico," Drury File, BBNP, RG 79, NA.

31. Presnall to Devereaux Butcher, November 26, 1945, NPS Files, BBIP, RG 79, NA.

32. Minchen to Morelock, January 21, 1947, NPS Files, BBIP, RG 79, NA.

33. "Report on the Study Made in La Sierra del Carmen, Coahuila, for the Creation of an International Park between the United States and Mexico," Drury File, BBNP, RG 79, NA.

July 1947 and subsequently obtained a promise from the Mexican representatives that their country would initiate a decree establishing Parque Nacional de la Gran Comba, the new name for the Mexican portion of the park.[34]

This development suddenly alarmed Americans who owned or leased property on the Mexican side of the Rio Grande. Their concerns related to the belief that if the park became a reality, they would not be compensated properly for their holdings.[35] Pressure on their part ultimately forced the State Department to instruct United States consulates in Chihuahua, Coahuila, and Sonora that this country would have no cause for apprehension provided that Mexican officials would not "interfere with the normal cattle grazing or agricultural pursuits of American citizens owning or controlling lands in the area."[36] The value of American mining, cattle, and other enterprises in the Mexican border states of Sonora, Coahuila, and Chihuahua totaled several million dollars. The American Club, a sportsmen's organization with headquarters in San Antonio, controlled 100,000 acres "in probably the most beautiful part of the lovely Carmen Mountains."[37] It also contained vast timber resources which probably would be encompassed within the Mexican park.[38]

In December 1947, Assistant Park Service Director Hillory Tolson wrote Carlos Villas Perez, a member of the international com-

---

34. Garrison, "A History of the Proposed Big Bend International Park," July 6, 1953 (revised April 1, 1954), BBNP Lib.

35. John A. Loomis to Tolson, July 22, 1947, NPS Files, BBIP, RG 79, NA.

36. American interests were also concerned about the possible establishment of other international projects in Mexico. M. L. Stafford to Stephen E. Aguirre, September 5, 1947, NPS Files, BBIP, RG 79, NA. Aguirre was American Consul at Ciudad Juarez. Carbon copies of the above were sent to the American Consuls in Agua Prieta, Sonora; Chihuahua, Chihuahua; Nogales, Sonora; Piedras Negras, Coahuila.

37. Ernest Marsh, Jr., "A Preliminary Report on a Biological Survey of the Santa Rosa and Del Carmen Mountains of Northern Coahuila, Mexico," October 11, 1936, File 702-04, BBNP, RG 79, NA.

38. American Embassy in Mexico's Despatch Number 4790, "Development of International Parks in Big Bend and Coronado International Memorial Areas," October 6, 1947, NPS Files, BBIP, RG 79, NA. Dolph and Mason Briscoe of Uvalde, Texas controlled the Rosita Livestock Company, another American owned enterprise.

mission. Tolson asked the Mexican official most actively working for the national park to consider the possibility of authorizing leases for the American land owners so that they could "continue to graze cattle or carry on other enterprises." He likewise mentioned that these holdings should not "interfere too greatly with the preservation of the park area."[39] Tolson's letter came at the time when the Park Service was trying to purchase all the remaining privately owned lands within Big Bend National Park. Evidently, the Service could operate on a double standard when American interests were involved in a foreign country. But Mexico gave no encouragement to the proposal. By December 1948 the State Department dropped the idea after concluding that certain American interests would be "adversely affected" by any decrees from Mexico concerning the Big Bend and Coronado international projects.[40]

The antipathy that many Americans, especially Texans, traditionally displayed toward Mexico's cultural heritage constituted another source of friction. Several Park Service reports, for instance, had emphasized the unique Spanish-Mexican atmosphere of the Big Bend area and one report even proposed that the architecture of the park buildings reflect this fact.[41] But because of the objections of several prominent Texans, the Park Service would delete a para-

---

39. Tolson to Carlos Villas Perez, December 18, 1947, NPS Files, BBIP, RG 79, NA.

40. Assistant Secretary of State to Secretary of the Interior, November 26, 1947, NPS Files, BBIP, RG 79, NA; Assistant Secretary of State to J. A. Krug, December 3, 1948, NPS Files, BBIP, RG 79, NA. The State Department agreed with the opinion of the American Embassy in Mexico City that "the Mexican Government will expropriate whatever part of the aforementioned properties may fall within the boundaries of the proposed Mexican National Parks, once they are delineated, whether the interests concerned are owned by American or Mexican citizens. The past action of the Mexican Government in such matters indicate that any private interests which may be in conflict with what is considered the National interest will not be held worthy of consideration."

41. "Report of the Big Bend Area, Texas," January, 1935, File 207, BBNP, RG 79, NA; J. D. Coffman, "Report on the Forest and Vegetation Aspect," August 9, 1935, File 0-32, Part. I, BBNP, RG 79, NA; Maier to State Park ECW, June 8, 1935, File 0-32, Part I, BBNP, RG 79, NA; NPS Press Release, March 3, 1935, File 0-32, Part I, BBNP, RG 79, NA; Bernard F. Manbey, "Proposed Big Bend National Park Report on Suggested Park Boundary, Engineering Requirements and General Notes," August 19, 1935, File 0-32, Part IX, BBNP, RG 79, NA.

graph in a press release which referred to this aspect.[42] Today, none of the major structures in the park shows any Mexican architectural influence except for the tile roofs on some of the lodge houses in the Chisos Basin.

Another instance of anti-Mexican sentiment occurred in 1947 when United States Senator Tom Connally called for the construction of a fence along the Rio Grande border of Big Bend National Park to keep out Mexican livestock and wildlife allegedly infected with hoof and mouth disease.[43] Previously, A. W. Dorgan, a self-appointed apostle for an international park for world peace, emphasized that if his proposed Pan American Highway were built through the park, the United States could rush troops and armaments down the road and easily subdue Mexico if the need arose.[44] Attitudes such as these obviously did not provide a favorable climate for the consummation of a "friendly nations" park.

The Korean conflict and the Cold War kept negotiations between the United States and Mexico at a standstill, but efforts continued at the local level. At the encouragement of Big Bend's new superintendent, Lon Garrison, the Alpine Chamber of Commerce revived the international park project in 1953 and formed its own peace park commission. Local educators and businessmen with a few prominent individuals from Chihuahua, Coahuila, and various West Texas cities composed its membership. In September of that year, Superintendent Garrison and other members of the Alpine commission discussed the international project with several Mexican officials and businessmen at Saltillo, Coahuila. One month later Garrison's group flew to Chihuahua City to meet with the local state governor. Other sessions occurred on both sides of the border, but except for the continued enthusiasm over the idea of an international park, the results were limited.[45]

In November 1955, Secretary of the Interior Douglas McKay

---

42. Isabelle F. Story memorandum to William E. Warne, June 26, 1943, File 501, BBNP, RG 79, NA.

43. Chicago *Daily News*, January 29, 1947.

44. Dorgan to Ickes, October 8, 1934, File 0-32, Part I, BBNP, RG 79, NA.

45. Garrison, "A History of the Proposed Big Bend International Park," July 6, 1953 (revised April 1, 1954), BBNP Lib.

delivered the dedication speech for Big Bend National Park. The ceremony had been postponed several times since 1944 because of global conflicts. McKay optimistically stated that the work of the various commissions would eventually make the international park a reality: "The pooling and mutual sharing of great scenic treasures along those borders is an inspiring example to the troubled peoples behind the iron and bamboo curtains of the way free men and women can live in peace and friendship."[46] But events would prove that it takes more than rhetoric to bring about the establishment of an international park.

Continued visitations, meetings, and assorted activities in behalf of the international park followed, but another significant event did not occur until 1963. In that year Roberto Garduno Garcia, Director of Forestry and National Parks in Mexico, visited Big Bend and indicated that his government planned to establish and develop a Mexican park on the Rio Grande.[47] Conrad Wirth, Director of the United States Park Service, told Garcia that the proposed international project represented another step that would bring Mexico and the United States closer together.[48] Still, nothing concrete came from either statement.

President Luis Echevaria of Mexico in 1971 once again revived the idea of Parque Nacional de la Gran Comba when he ordered his Department of Tourism to investigate the proposal, to formulate plans, and to carry out the project. The United States Park Service rushed detailed information to Mexico City. And even though the Department of Tourism in Mexico City would eventually complete a report on the international park concept, nothing yet has occurred.[49]

Thus, after half a century the international park on the Rio

---

46. Dedication Speech for Big Bend National Park by Douglas McKay, November 21, 1955, BBNP Lib.

47. Giving some substance to critics's charges that Mexico did not comprehend United States Park Service policies were the frequent name changes of the agency that oversees Mexico's national parks. The most at odds semantically was the Department of Forestry and Hunting.

48. W. J. Newell to the author, April 26, 1973.

49. *Ibid.* An Associate Director of the Park Service wrote in spring of 1973 that "Mexico has taken no further action" on the park proposal, an indication that the Park Service considers Mexico responsible for the delay. Stanley W. Hulett to the author, April 4, 1973.

Grande is still far from a reality. Recent developments on the United States-Mexican border such as the settlement of the Chamizal controversy and the cooperative effort which produced the Falcon Dam and Amistad Reservoirs hopefully foreshadow the eventual creation of Big Bend International Park. However, Mexico's concept of national parks still remains at odds with that of the United States National Park Service. In a country where needed resources have not yet been tapped, especially in the northern extremes of the Chihuahuan Desert, scenic preservation remains of secondary importance. During the 1960s the Big Bend area has become more significant from an economic perspective as visitors to the park increased from approximately 76,000 in 1960 to almost 300,000 in 1972. This possibly caused Mexico to renew efforts toward establishing a sister park opposite Big Bend. But the energy stortages that developed in 1973 and restrictions on automobile travel doubtless will have an adverse and long-range effect on the park's tourist business. The wilderness proposal could also discourage increased tourism and mean less improvements and developments other than for hikers and tent campers. Since Mexico has shown a tendency to develop the lands adhacent to Big Bend for greater economic potential, the international park possibly will be delayed indefinitely.[50]

---

50. A letter to the author from J. F. Carithers, Superintendent, BBNP, August 14, 1975 reflects the current thinking of the NPS on the matter: "If and when the land is actually set aside, the Mexican park and Big Bend will probably be regarded as companion parks, rather than as a single international park. The resources of the two areas would certainly complement each other, and provide visitors from both countries with an outstanding experience." The 1973 master plan likewise stresses the "companion park" concept. *Big Bend National Park Master Plan* (Washington, D. C.: Department of the Interior/National Park Service, 1973), pp. 32–33.

Epilogue

As we have seen, Big Bend National Park was a product of the Great Depression. Although there had been previous efforts to secure a national park for Texas, a determined effort did not take place until the 1930s. Resolutions from the Texas Legislature, the State Democratic convention, and the governor requested the federal government to establish at least one national park in the Lone Star State to help ease unemployment.

In 1933 State Representatives R. M. Wagstaff (Abilene) and E. E. Townsend (Alpine) introduced House Bill 771 in the Texas Legislature. It easily passed and the act created Texas Canyons State Park on fifteen sections of land in the vicinity of Santa Elena, Mariscal, and Boquillas Canyons on the Rio Grande in southern Brewster County. Later that year the name was changed to Big Bend State Park and the Chisos Mountains were added to the park acreage.

The National Park Service investigated the site in January 1934 to determine its suitability for a Civilian Conservation Corps camp. Roger Toll, Superintendent of Yellowstone and chief investigator of the NPS, not only recommended it for a CCC camp, but also considered it an ideal site for a national park. He regarded Big Bend as "decidedly the outstanding scenic area of Texas."

In March 1935, U. S. Representative Ewing Thomason and U. S. Senators Morris Sheppard and Tom Connally introduced legislation in the House and Senate to establish Big Bend National Park. It passed with virtually no local or congressional opposition and became law on June 20, 1935. President Franklin D. Roosevelt strongly supported the measure partly because of the possibility of an international park on the Rio Grande which would further his "Good Neighbor" policy with Mexico.

In fall 1935 the two countries began discussions regarding the international project. Subsequent meetings have been held over the years, but no real progress has been made with both sides blaming the other for the stalemate. The United States has criticized Mexico for permitting logging and private developments in its national parks, practices contrary to U. S. Park Service policies. Mexico, on the other hand, contended that Americans had established a park at Big Bend because the land was worthless for any other use.

Land acquisition presented several problems in Big Bend. When Texas entered the Union, it retained ownership of its public lands, many acres of which were sold to private investors. In addition, the Texas Permanent School Fund controlled the mineral rights in the Big Bend Country. Fortunately for the park project, exhaustive geological studies proved that the mineral worth of the land was minimal. Next, state and local boosters undertook two unsuccessful fund raising drives from 1937 to 1941. Eventually, most of the lands were purchased with a $1.5 million appropriation from the 47th Legislature. However, several thousand acres remained in private hands. Although the state had the obligation to present these to the federal government, it never did and Congress finally had to appropriate the funds, $300,375 for 8,561.75 acres. By 1972 the entire park area of 708,118.40 acres was in federal ownership.

It has been over half a century since Congress passed the enabling legislation for Big Bend, yet it still remains one of the best kept secrets in the national park system. Although considerably more Texans (as well as others) know of the region than the one per cent E. E. Townsend estimated in the 1930s, Big Bend has never had the visitation of the major western parks. In 1976, the year of the nation's bicentennial, 456,161 visitors were counted, a record for the desert park, but a paltry sum indeed when compared with the 2,753,020 at Yosemite or the 2,525,040 at Yellowstone. In fact, annual visitation to Big Bend has never reached 500,000, the figure projected by the NPS. Boosters who hoped for increased revenues from tourism blamed the agency's policies of minimal development and designation of over seventy-five percent of the park area as wilderness. In addition, the oil shortage that began in Fall 1973 temporarily reduced automobile travel throughout the United States. But the greatest obstacle to increased visitation to Big Bend is its geographical isolation. The nearest major city, El Paso, is over 300 miles away. From Fort Stockton on Interstate 10 (the freeway between San Antonio and El Paso), the Persimmon Gap park entrance is 127 miles distant. Even Yellowstone, located in the northwestern corner of Wyoming, has greater accessibility with Interstate 90 in Montana only sixty-nine miles from its northern entrance at Gardiner and Mammoth Hot Springs.

Despite the disappointment of some, the isolation of the park had a potential advantage. Except for severe overgrazing, the area was relatively unaffected by man's presence. This provided the NPS the unique opportunity to develop a comprehensive master plan in which proven policies could be implemented. Such a plan was available during the 1940s when Big Bend first opened its gates. Unfortunately, for over a decade the development of the park was dictated by economic conditions, pressures from local boosters, and the recreational whims of the public rather than sound, long-range planning. Visitors enjoyed the coolness of the Chisos Mountains during the summer and the range consequently became the major tourist overnight spot in the park. This occurred despite the views of several Service experts that too many people would harm the fragile ecology of the Chisos Basin, a principal scenic attraction. In 1971 the Service finally drew up a master plan similar in many ways to the earlier version that placed the major visitor improvements and services on the Rio Grande. Perhaps now Big Bend can actually realize the dual national park purposes of use for the present and preservation of the natural and historic resources for future generations without either seriously infringing on the other.

Appendix

Map of Big Bend National Park

Public No. 157–74th Congress [S. 2131]

Big Bend National Park Chronology

Official Annual Visitation Figures for Big Bend, 1944–1985

Visits to U. S. National Parks, 1976–1977

Summary of Responses to Wilderness Recommendation

Select List of Decimal Classifications, Record Group 79

BIG BEND NATIONAL PARK
BREWSTER COUNTY, TEXAS

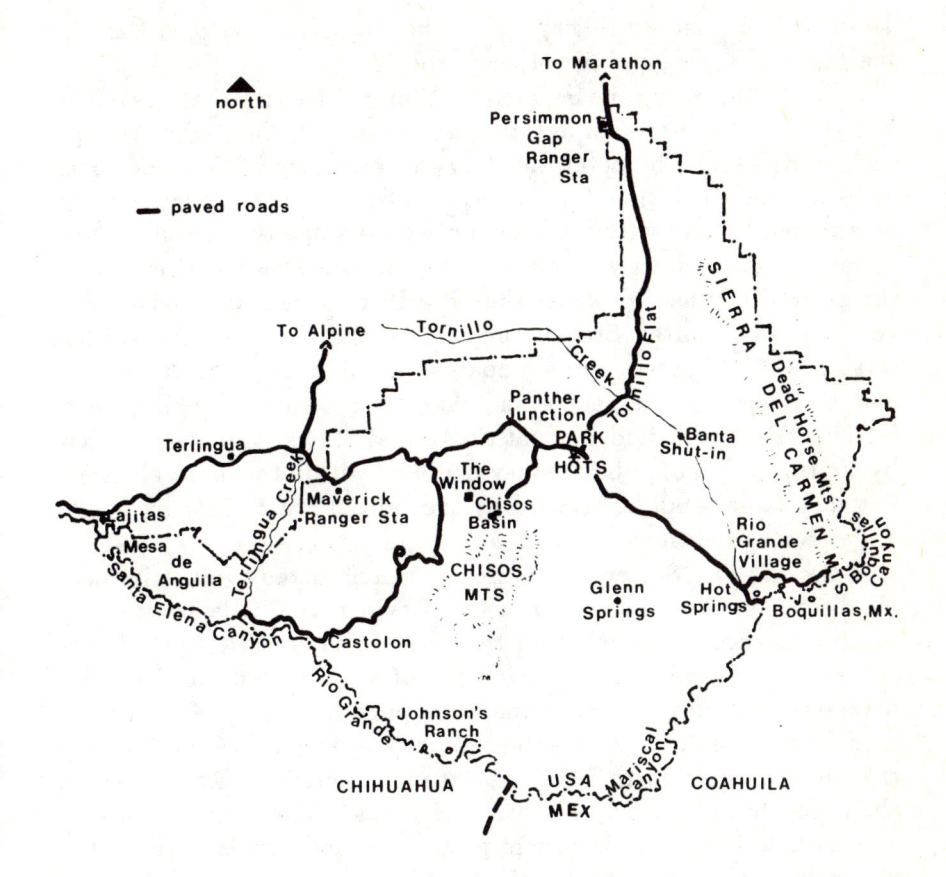

[Public No. 157–74th Congress]
[S. 2131]

AN ACT

To provide for the establishment of the Big Bend National Park in the State of Texas, and for other purposes.

Be it enacted by the Senate and House of Representatives of the United States of America in Congress assembled, That when title to such lands as may be determined by the Secretary of the Interior as necessary for recreational park purposes within the boundaries to be determined by him within the area of approximately one million five hundred thousand acres, in the counties of Brewster and Presidio, in the State of Texas, known as the "Big Bend" area, shall have been vested in the United States, such lands shall be, and are hereby, established, dedicated, and set apart as a public park for the benefit and enjoyment of the people and shall be known as the "Big Bend National Park": Provided, That the United States shall not purchase by appropriation of public money and land within the aforesaid area, but such lands shall be secured by the United States only by public and private donations.

Sec. 2. The Secretary of the Interior is hereby authorized, in his discretion and upon submission of evidence of title satisfactory to him, to accept, on behalf of the United States, title to the lands referred to in the previous section hereof as may be deemed by him necessary or desirable for national-park purposes: Provided, That no land for said park shall be accepted until exclusive jurisdiction over the entire area, in form satisfactory to the Secretary of the Interior, shall have been ceded by the State of Texas to the United States.

Sec. 3. The administration, protection, and development of the aforesaid park shall be excercised under the direction of the Secretary of the Interior by the National Park Service, subject to the provisions of the Act of August 25, 1916 (39 Stat. 535), entitled "An Act to establish a National Park Service, and for other purposes" as amended: Provided, That the provisions of the Act of June 10, 1920, known as the "Federal Water Power Act", shall not apply to this park.

Approved, June 20, 1935.

Appendix

Big Bend National Park Chronology

1931

Senate Concurrent Resolution 9 called for an immediate survey to determine if Texas' scenic areas measured up to national park qualifications

1933

January–Texas National Park dropped from Park Service list of proposed park sites

February–R. M. Wagstaff, Abilene and E. E. Townsend, Alpine introduce bill in state legislature for creation of Texas Canyons State Park

May 27–Texas Canyons State Park bill passed

October 27–Texas Canyons changed to Big Bend State Park and acreage increased to include Chisos Mountains

1934

January–Roger Toll of the NPS investigated Big Bend State Park

March–Report prepared by Toll recommended national park status for Big Bend

May–Director Arno B. Cammerer approved Big Bend National Park Project; CCC camp opened in the Chisos Basin

1935

January–Second NPS report on Big Bend included first mention of idea for international park

February–United States Senator Morris Sheppard wrote President Franklin D. Roosevelt regarding international park proposal

March 4–United States Representative Ewing Thomason and Senators Sheppard and Tom Connally introduced bill to create Big

Bend National Park

June 20–Big Bend enabling legislation becomes law

October and November–Two conferences held with Mexican and United States representatives regarding the international park

1937

May–Walter Prescott Webb float trip through Santa Elena Canyon

June–Governor James V. Allred vetoed $750,000 appropriation bill

July–First fund raising campaign under auspices of Local Park Committees

Fall–45th Texas Legislature authorized Texas State Parks Board to receive donations of land and money for Big Bend

December–CCC camp closed

1938

May–Second fund raising campaign organized under direction of Amon Carter's Texas Big Bend Park Association

1939

May–Mineral rights Permanent School Fund relinquished by 46th Legislature

1940

CCC camp reestablished

1941

July–47th Legislature appropriated $1,500,000 for Big Bend land purchase

September–Texas State Parks Board and Big Bend Land Department began land acquisition.

1943

September 5–Title to Big Bend lands presented to NPS

1944

June 6–Deed of Cession presented to President Roosevelt

June 12–Big Bend National Park officially established

July–NPS assumed operation of Big Bend; Ross Maxwell was the first superintendent

1946

June–National Park Concessions, Inc. began operation of the concessions franchise

1947

May–First Ranger campfire program given

December–Rancher concern over park as a "predator incubator"

1949

August–Saddle horse rides offered for the first time

1952

Ross Maxwell resigned

1955

November 21–Big Bend National Park dedication; Secretary of the Interior Douglas McKay gave the dedication speech

1956–66

Mission 66

1966

April–Mrs. Lyndon B. Johnson and Secretary of the Interior Stewart L. Udall visited the national park

1976

During the nation's bicentennial year, 456,201 visit the park, a record

Table 1
Official Annual Visitation Figures for Big Bend

Calendar Year	Visitors
1944	1,409
1945	3,205
1946	10,037
1947	28,652
1948	45,670
1949	62,150
1950	70,325
1951	84,051
1952	94,367
1953	86,635
1954	67,280
1955	80,990
1956	89,709
1957	74,960
1958	72,630
1959	70,370
1960	75,870
1961	90,565
1962	90,972
1963	114,232
1964	119,698
1965	174,566
1966	163,548
1967	173,290
1968	191,764
1969	199,805
1970	172,648
1971	247,401
1972	290,245
1973	341,273
1974	191,252
1975	331,913
1976	456,201
1977	402,433
1978	362,888

1979	339,690
1980	209,650
1981	201,603
1982	217,038
1983	198,708
1984	202,005
1985	227,261

Table 2
Visits to U.S. National Parks, 1976–77*

National Park	1976	1977
Acadia(ME)	2,775,137	3,181,269
Arches(UT)	294,742	313,383
Big Bend(TX)	456,161	402,433
Bryce Canyon(UT)	626,074	612,768
Canyonlands(UT)	79,978	75,591
Capitol Reef (UT)	469,737	467,953
Carlsbad Caverns (NM)	876,500	862,784
Crater Lake (OR)	606,457	617,482
Everglades (FL)	1,032,613	1,067,767
Glacier (MT)	1,662,727	1,656,212
Gt. Smoky Mtns (NC-TN)	11,421,800	11,621,606
Grand Canyon (AZ)	3,026,389	2,848,519
Grand Teton (WY)	3,856,900	3,973,642
Guadalupe Mtns (TX)	81,347	92,189
Haleakala (HI)	669,136	651,138
Hawaii Volcanoes (HI)	1,852,600	1,816,836
Hot Springs (AR)	4,737,800	5,152,047
Isle Royale (MI)	16,964	16,676
Kings Canyon (CA)	1,133,606	1,046,614
Lassen Volcanic (CA)	461,600	381,157
Mammoth Cave (KY)	1,921,700	1,979,351
Mesa Verde (CO)	676,928	664,894
Mount McKinley (AK)	519,484	507,598
Mount Rainier (WA)	1,972,113	2,437,332
North Cascades (WA)	769,295	689,679
Olympic (WA)	2,672,800	2,658,922
Petrified Forest (AZ)	1,074,529	865,565
Redwood (CA)	442,288	510,744
Rocky Mountain (CO)	2,741,544	2,894,994
Sequoia (CA)	1,041,614	978,573
Shenandoah (VA)	2,715,000	3,055,000
Virgin Islands (VI)	315,408	454,708
Voyageurs (MN)	121,154	140,255
Wind Cave (SD)	930,521	1,051,607
Yellowstone (WY-MT-ID)	2,525,040	2,487,084

Yosemite (CA)	2,753,020	2,535,846
Zion (UT)	1,222,205	1,209,649

Statistical Abstract, 1977 (Washington, D. C.: Department of the Interior/National Park Service, 1979), pp. 23–24.

Summary of Responses Received
to 1973 Wilderness Recommendation
for Big Bend National Park*

Recommendation	Public Agencies	Private Organizations	Individuals	Total
National Park Service Proposal	3	35	2265	2303
Enlarge NPS Proposal	2	24	684	710
Reduce NPS Proposal	11	10	305	326
Wilderness; No Specific Recommendations	3	7	2053	2063
No Wilderness	16	15	58	89
Acknowledgements Received with No Specific Comments on Wilderness Proposal	7	1	5	13
TOTALS	42	92	5370	5504

**Wilderness Recommendation: Big Bend National Park, Texas,* (Washington, D. C.: Department of the Interior/National Park Service, 1973), p. 27.

Appendix

Select List of Decimal Classifications Used in the Central Classified Files, Record Group 79

000 General
    0-1 Conferences
        0-1.1   Superintendents
        0-1.2   Rangers
        0-1.4   Staff
        0-1.5   Operators
    0-3 Invitations and Address
    0-5 Records and Files
    0-10 Laws and Legal Matters (General)
        0-10.1   Decisions of Attorney General
        0-10.2   Decisions of Comptroller
        0-10.3   Decisions of Solicitor
    0-15 Final Opinions and Orders
    0-20 Executive Departments and Establishments
    0-30 Foreign Parks
    0-31 Military Parks
    0-32 Proposed Parks
    0-33 State Parks
    0-35 Proposed Monuments
    0-36 Proposed National Historical Parks
    0-37 Proposed National Military Parks
    0-38 Parkways
    0-39 Biological Wild Life Preserves
    0-40 Recreational Areas
    0-42 Memorials

100 History and Legislation
    101 History (General)
        101-01   Dedications
    120 Legislation
        120-01   House bills
        120-02   Senate bills
        120-05   Acts

200 Administration and Personnel
  201 Administration (General)
     201-01   Director
     201-02   Associate Director
     201-03   Assistant Director
       201-03.1 General Superintendent and Landscape Engineer
     201-04   Regional Directors
     201-06   Superintendents and Custodians
       201-06.1 Assistant Superintendents
     201-10   U.S. Commissioners
     201-12   Inspectors
     201-13   Organization
       201-13.1 Organization charts
     201-14   Reorganization
     201-15   Policy
  204 Inspections and Investigations (General)
     204-01   By congressional committees
     204-10   By field officers
     204-20   By headquarters officers
  205 Instructions and Orders (General)
     205-01   Executive Orders
       205-01.1 Proclamations
     205-02   National Park Service
     205-03   Secretary's
  206 Mail Facilities (General)
     206-08   Post offices (establishment of)
  207 Reports (General)
     207-01   Annual
       207-01.2 Director's
       207-01.3 Secretary's
       207-01.4 Superintendents'
       207-01.5 Park Naturalist's
     207-02   Monthly
       207-02.1 Director's
       207-02.3 Superintendents'
     207-03   Historians'
     207-04   Park Naturalist's
     207-05   Rangers'

Appendix

  207-20 Weather
  207-22 Final construction reports
  207-23 Burials
 208 Rules and Regulations (General)
  208-01 Automobile and motorcycles
   208-01.1 Drivurself
   208-01.2 License
   208-01.3 Fees
   208-01.4 Permits
  208-05 Drumming
  208-06 Fishing, hunting, and trapping
  208-08 Liquor traffic
  208-09 Livestock
  208-10 Moral conditions
  208-11 Robbery
  208-30 Uniforms and equipment
  208-40 Vandalism
  208-41 Deaths
  208-43 Mining
  208-44 Firearms
  208-47 Sales tax
 250 Personal
 252 Employment
 256 Examinations
 257 Leave

300 Appropriations, Finance, and Accounts
 302 Appropriations - Estimates (General)
 303 Appropriations (General)
  303-02 Donations
  303-03 Emergency reconstruction and forest fires
  303-05 Insect infestations
  303-13 Claims, settlement of
 305 Disbursing Clerk (General)
 306 Accounts (General)
 307 Receipts and Revenues (General)

400 Supplies and Equipment
   403 Contracts
      403-01   Contracts correspondence
      403-02   Contractors
   405 Inventories
   425 Books, Magazines, Etc.
   432 Forms and Stationery (General)
   435 Gasoline and Oils (General)
   443 Motor and Steam Equipment
      443-14   Boats
   444 Photographic Equipment Supplies
   455 Uniforms and Equipment

500 Publicity and Statistics
   501 Publicity
      501-01   Advertising
      501-02   Magazine articles
      501-03   Newspaper articles (press notices)
      501-04   Special articles on national parks (speeches)
   502 Entertainments and Lectures
   503 Pictures (General)
      503-10   Moving pictures (General)
   504 Publications (General)
      504-01   Bulletins
      504-03   Manuals
      504-04   Maps
         504-04.1 Motorist guides
         504-04.2 Blueprints
      504-07   Portfolio of National Parks
      504-11   [*Nature Notes*]
   550 Statistics (General)

600 Lands, Buildings, Roads, and Trails
      600-01   Master plan
      600-02   Six-year program
      600-03   Development outline
      600-04   Specifications

601 Lands (General)
    601-01   Administration sites
    601-02   Airfield sites
    601-03   Camp sites
    601-05   Reservoir sites
    601-09   Cemetery sites
    601-11   Park entrances
    601-12   Recreational areas
    601-13   Wilderness areas
    601-14   Research preserves
    601-15   Landscaping
    601-18   Soil and moisture
602 Boundaries (General)
    602-01   Boundaries (extension)
603 Condemning of Lands
604 Donations
605 Entries
    605-01   Exchanges
    605-02   School lands
606 Irrigation (General)
607 Jurisdiction (General)
608 Memorials (General)
609 Leases
    609-01   Mining claims
610 Private Holdings (General)
    610-01   Purchasing of lands (precedent for)
    610-02   Taxes
611 Repairs and Improvements
    611-01   Elevators
612 Rights of Way
613 Sale of Lots
614 Surveys
615 Value of Lands
616 Withdrawals and Restorations
618 Public Works Administration
619 Civil Works Administration (FERA and SERA)
620 Buildings (General)
    620-01   Administration building
    620-08   Checking stations

        620-10   Churches
        620-20   Community buildings
        620-30   Fish hatchery
        620-31   Gauging stations
        620-36   Hospitals
        620-37   Lookout stations
        620-46   Museums
        620-49   Observatories
        620-51   Post offices
        620-53   Power houses
        620-54   Pump houses
        620-63   **Ranger cabins and stations**
        620-68   Schools
        620-80   Shelter cabins
621 Construction Projects
630 Roads (General)
    630-02   Maintenance
        630-02.1 Oiling
        630-02.2 Snow removal
631 Construction under Road Budget Program
    631-01   Roads budget—allotments
    631-02   Roads budget
632 Roads Outside of Park (Approach Roads)
633 Roadside Cleanup
640 Trails (General)
650 Lakes, Rivers, and Waterways
    650-01   Lakes
    650-02   Rivers
    650-03   Waterways
    650-04   Bridges
    650-05   Structures in waters
660 Plants and Systems
    660-03   Sanitary systems
    660-04   Telephone, telegraph and radio service
    660-05   Water supply systems (general)
        660-05.1 Distribution of
        660-05.2 Fountains
        660-05.4 Reservoirs
            660-05.41 Hetch Hetchy (San Francisco water

supply)
        660-05.5 Water analysis (mineral water)
          660-05.51 Radioactivity
        660-05.6 Water power
        660-05.7 Water rights
        660-05.8 Wells

700 Flora, Fauna, Natural Phenomena, Antiquities, and Sciences
    700-01   Nature study
  701 Flora (General)
      701-01.4 Trees
  710 Fauna
  713 Birds
  714 Fishes
  715 Mammals
      715-01   Antelope
      715-02   Bears
      715-03   Buffalo
      715-04   Deer
      715-05   Elk
      715-06   Goats and sheep
      715-07   Moose
      715-08   Beaver
  716 Insects (Arthropoda)
  717 Invertebrates (Except Arthropoda)
  718 Ecology
  719 Predatory Animals
  720 Protection and Care
      720-01   Feeding
      720-03   Preserves
      720-04   Wildlife survey
  721 Industry (General)
      721-02   Skins
  730 Natural Phenomena (General)
  731 Geography (General)
      731-01   Place names
      731-02   Topography of parks

732 Geology (General)
    732-03   Rocks minerals
        732-03.1 Requests for specimens
    732-06   Water
        732-06.1 Ice and glaciers
        732-06.2 Soil erosion and control
        732-06.5 Thermal phenomena (geysers)
        732-06.6 Underground water and caves
        732-06.7 Earth movements (including seismology)
        732-06.8 Vulcanism
740 Antiquities (General)
    740-01   Anthropology
    740-02   Archaeology
        740-02.1 Discoveries
        740-02.2 Relics
        740-02.3 Researches
    740-03   Ruins protection
750 Sciences (General)

800 Protection, Service to Public, and Forestry
    801 Protection (General)
        801-01   Accident
        801-02   Flood
        801-03   Policing
        801-04   Storms
        801-05   Fire
    831 Conventions (General)
    832 Expositions (General)
    833 Exhibits (General)
        833-01   Botanical
        833-02   Conservation of natural resources (including restorations)
        833-05   Museums
        833-07   Models
    834 Gifts Other Than Money (Donations)
    840 Educational Activities
        840-02.1 Bibliographies
        840-02.2 Libraries

840-02.3 Universities and colleges
843 Instruction (General)
    843-01   Courses of instruction in national parks conducted by outside institutions
    843-03   School facilities
    843-04   Special training
845 Research (General)
855 Medical Service (General)
857 Travel (General)
    857-01   Air travel
    857-04   Hotels and dude ranches
    857-06   Mountain climbing
    857-07   Opening of parks
    857-08   Railroads
867 Tours (General)
868 Winter Sports
871 (870-1) Associations, Clubs and Committees
880 Forestry (General)
    883 Forest Protection (General)
        883-01   Fires
        883-02   Protection improvements
        883-03   Fire records
            883-03.1 Individual fire reports
            883-03.3 Annual reports (fire)
        883-06   Insect infestations
        883-07   Forest protection cooperation
            883-07.1 Forest Protection Board
    884 Forest Products (General)
        884-03   Timber
            884-03.1 Sale of forest timber
    885 Silviculture
        885-01   Emergency Conservation Work: Civilian Conservation Corps, Reforestation

900 Concessions
  900 Public Utility Operators
    900-01   Buildings

900-02 Contracts
900-03 Financial reports
900-04 Lands
900-05 Miscellaneous correspondence
900-06 Rates
900-07 Reports (semimonthly)
900-08 Complaints
901 Privileges and Permits
901-01 Grazing permits

Bibliography

Primary Materials

Special Collections

Big Bend National Park File, Amon Carter Museum, Fort Worth, Texas.
Big Bend National Park Land Acquisition File, Texas Parks and Wildlife Department, Austin, Texas.
Park Records at Big Bend National Park, Texas.
Records of Big Bend National Park, Record Group 79, National Archives Building, Washington, D. C.
Records of Big Bend State Park, Bastrop State Park Warehouse, Bastrop, Texas.
Records of Newton B. Drury, Director's Personal File, Big Bend National Park, 1940 to March, 1951, Record Group 79, National Archives Building, Washington, D. C.
Records of the National Park Service, Central Classified Files, 1907–1949, File 0-32, Big Bend Proposed International Park, Part I, Record Group 79, National Archives Building, Washington, D. C.
Records of the Office of the Secretary of the Interior, National Parks, Big Bend, Texas, General, Part II, Record Group 48, National Archives Building, Washington, D. C.
Walter Prescott Webb Papers, General Correspondence, 1937, Eugene C. Barker Texas History Center, University of Texas, Austin, Texas.
Walter Prescott Webb Papers, Texas State Archives, Austin, Texas.

Correspondence

Letters to author from Joe Brown, Assistant Director, National Park Service, November 23, 1973; December 13, 1973; January 10, 1974.

Letters to author from J. F. Carithers, Superintendent, Big Bend National Park, December 6, 1973; August 14, 1975.

Letter to author from Clifford B. Casey, Alpine, Texas, February 21, 1973.

Letters to author from Bill M. Collins, Head, Concession Management and Contracts Section, Texas Parks and Wildlife Department, May 23, 1973; August 16, 1973; November 6, 1973.

Letters to author from Stanley W. Hulett, Associate Director, National Park Service, April 4, 1973; May 7, 1973.

Letters to author from Ross A. Maxwell, Austin, Texas, October 2, 1972; May 17, 1973; August 6, 1973.

Letter to author from Robert C. Morris, Acting Superintendent, Big Bend National Park, April 4, 1973.

Letters to author from W. J. Newell, Alpine, Texas, April 26, 1973; December 5, 1974.

Letter to author from Myron D. Sutton, Acting Chief, Division of International Park Affairs, National Park Service, May 24, 1974.

Letter to author from Charles P. Torrey, Director, Office of Mexican Affairs, Department of State, May 15, 1974.

Letters to author from Robert Wear, Arlington, Texas, July 8, 1972; July 27, 1972.

Letters to author from Caroline C. Wilson, Park Technician, Big Bend National Park, August 19, 1973; September 14, 1973.

Interviews

Personal Interview with Ross A. Maxwell, Austin, Texas, December 21, 1972.

Personal Interview with Ronnie C. Tyler, Curator of History, Amon Carter Museum, Fort Worth, Texas, October 10, 1973.

Personal Interview with Robert Wear, Arlington, Texas, September 21, 1972.

Bibliography

Public Documents

Journal of the Senate of Texas. 1931; 1933; 1939
U. S. *Congressional Record.* XLII; XLVII; LIII; LV; LXV; LXXI; LXXIV; LXXIX.
U. S. *Statutes at Large.* XLIX; LXIII; IXVII; LXXVII.
Vernon's Texas Statutes. 1948.

Newspapers

Abilene *Reporter-News.* 1938; 1944.
Albuquerque *Journal.* 1939.
Alexandria, Louisiana *Town Talk.* 1944.
Alpine *Avalanche.* 1936–1939; 1942; 1945;
Amarillo *Daily News.* 1938.
Amarillo *News.* 1939.
Austin *American.* 1936.
Austin *Daily Texan.* 1937.
Austin *Dispatch.* 1937.
Austin *State Observer.* 1939.
Austin *Statesman.* 1937; 1939.
Austin *Times.* 1939.
Balmorhea *Texan.* 1939.
Brownwood *Bulletin.* 1937.
Butte, Montana *Daily Post.* 1936.
Charleston, West Virginia *Gazette.* 1944.
Chicago *Daily News.* 1947.
Christian Science Monitor. 1936; 1944
Colorado City, Texas *Record.* 1939.
Corpus Christi *Caller-Times.* 1939.
Cumberland, Maryland *Times.* 1944.
Dallas *Dispatch-Journal.* 1939.
Dallas *Morning News.* 1936–1940; 1944–1945
Dallas *Times-Herald.* 1936–1939.
Del Rio *Evening News.* 1938.
Del Rio *Herald.* 1939.
Denver *Post.* 1936–1937.

Detroit, Michigan *News.* 1945.
Eden *Echo.* 1939.
El Paso *Herald-Post.* 1936–1938; 1947.
El Paso *Times.* 1935–1937; 1939; 1948.
Fort Stockton *Pioneer.* 1939.
Fort Worth *Star-Telegram.* 1936–1942; 1958.
Galveston *News.* 1938–1939.
Galveston *Tribune.* 1936–1937.
Goose Creek *Sun.* 1938.
Graham *Reporter.* 1939.
Harlingen *Valley Morning Star.* 1939.
Houston *Chronicle.* 1937.
Houston *Post.* 1937–1938.
Houston *Press.* 1937–1939; 1944.
Lufkin *Daily News.* 1937.
Mankato, Minnesota *Free Press.* 1944.
Marlin *Democrat.* 1939.
Marshall *News-Messenger.* 1939.
Miami, Florida *News.* 1941.
New York *Herald Tribune.* 1944.
New York *Times.* 1935.
Oakland, California *Tribune.* 1944.
Odessa *American.* 1972.
Oklahoma City *Oklahoman.* 1937.
Oklahoma City *Times.* 1937.
Palestine *Herald Press.* 1938.
Pecos *Enterprise.* 1938.
Philadelphia, Pennsylvania *Evening Public Ledger.* 1938.
Portsmouth, Virginia *Star.* 1944.
San Angelo *Standard-Times.* 1938–1939; 1947–1949.
San Antonio *Evening News.* 1938.
San Antonio *Express.* 1937–1939.
San Antonio *Light.* 1938.
San Antonio *News.* 1937.
San Francisco *Call Bulletin.* 1944.
Shamrock *Texan.* 1939.
Temple *Telegraph.* 1939.
Texarkana *News.* 1939.
Tyler *Morning Telegraph.* 1937; 1939.

Vernon *Record.* 1939.
Washington, D. C. *Star.* 1944.
Wichita Falls *Record News.* 1939.
Wichita Falls *Times.* 1939.
Woodville *Booster.* 1939.
Yoakum *Herald.* 1939.

Secondary Materials

Articles

Max Bentley. "Big Bend Park: Regional Executive Gets His First Look, Views It as 'Utterly Different' Among National Parks." *West Texas Today,* October, 1940, pp. 6–7.
"Big Bend, A Texas Wonderland is the Country's Newest National Park." *Life,* September 3, 1945, pp. 68–73.
"Big Bend is a National Park." *Parade,* March 28, 1948, pp. 19–21.
Glenn Burgess. "The Big Bend Deed is Passed." *West Texas Today,* September, 1943, pp. 6, 20.
C. B. Casey. "The Big Bend National Park." West Texas Historical and Scientific Society *Publication* No. 13 (1948).
——————. and Lewis H. Saxton. "The Life of Everett Ewing Townsend." West Texas Historical and Scientific Society *Publication* No. 17 (1958).
John N. Cole. "The Return of the Coyote." *Harper's Magazine,* CCXLVI (May, 1973), pp. 48–51.
Wayne Gard. "Where the Mountains Meet: The Big Bend Today." *Southwest Review,* XXVI (Winter, 1941), pp. 203–210.
Jean George. "What's Ahead for Our National Parks?" *National Wildlife,* X (February–March, 1972), pp. 36–41.
Harry Connelly. "Big Bend National Park Project Reality at Last." *West Texas Today,* September, 1941.
Cas Edwards. "Needed: A Good Dam." *Texas Game and Fish,* May, 1945, pp. 4–5.
Kenneth Foree, Jr. "Our New National Park on the Rio Grande." *Saturday Evening Post,* December 2, 1944, pp. 26–27, 106.
Robert T. Hill. "Dabs of Related Geology, Geography and History

along the Southwestern Border Region of the United States and Adjacent Mexico." *Texas Geographic*, I (May, 1937), pp. 26–34.

_____. "Running the Cañons of the Rio Grande: A Chapter of Recent Exploration." *Century Magazine*, LXI (January, 1901), pp. 371–387.

Jack Hope. "Big Bend: A Nice Place to Visit." *Audubon*, LXXV (July, 1973), pp. 36–49.

R. G. Ironside. "Private Development in National Parks: Residential and Commercial Facilities in the National Parks of North America." *Town Planning Review*, XVI (October, 1970), pp. 305–316.

John R. Jameson. "An International Peace Park on the Rio Grande: A Study of Cultural Differences," in *The American West: Essays in Honor of W. Eugene Hollon*, Ronald Lora, ed. Toledo, Ohio: University of Toledo Press, 1980.

_____. "The National Park System in the United States: An Overview with a Survey of Selected Government Documents and Archival Materials." *Government Publications Review*, VIIA (1980), pp. 145–158.

_____. "The Quest for a National Park in Texas." West Texas Historical Association *Year Book*, L (1974), pp. 47–60.

_____. "Walter Prescott Webb, Public Historian." *Public Historian*, VII (Spring, 1985), pp. 47–60.

Nathaniel T. Kenney. "Big Bend: Jewel in the Texas Desert." *National Geographic*, CXXXIII (January, 1968), pp. 104–133.

_____. "Our Wild and Scenic Rivers: The Rio Grande." *National Geographic*, CLII (July, 1977), pp. 46–51.

John Kord Lagemann. "Beauty on a Bend." *Collier's*, January 31, 1948, pp. 13–15, 67–68.

William J. Lawson and Will Mann Richardson. "The Texas State Park System: A History, Study of Development and Plans for the Future of the Texas State Parks." *Texas Geographic*, II (December, 1938), pp. 1–12.

George W. Long. "Many Splendored Glacierland." *National Geographic*, CIX (May, 1956), pp. 589–636.

Roderick Nash. "The American Invention of National Parks." *American Quarterly*, XXII (Fall, 1970), pp. 726–735.

Victor H. Schoffelmayer. "The Big Bend Area of Texas." *Texas Geographic*, I (May, 1937), pp. 1–25.

Frederick Simpich. "Down the Rio Grande: Taming this Strange, Turbulent Stream on Its Long Course from Colorado to the Gulf of Mexico." *National Geographic*, LXXVI (October, 1939), pp. 415–454.

Donald Swain. "The National Park Service and the New Deal, 1933–1940." *Pacific Historical Review*, XLI (August, 1972), pp. 312–332.

Minor R. Tillotson. "Newest National Park—Big Bend." *National Motorist*, June, 1945, pp. 10, 17–18.

"Roger Toll Obituary." *Trail and Timberline*, No. 209 (March–April, 1936), pp. 27–28.

Ronnie C. Tyler, ed. "Exploring the Rio Grande: Lt. Duff C. Green's Report of 1852." *Arizona and the West*, X (Spring, 1968), pp. 43–60.

Ronnie C. Tyler. "Robert T. Hill and the Big Bend: An 1889 Expedition that Helped Establish a Great National Park." *American West*, X (September, 1973), pp. 36–43.

R. M. Wagstaff. "Beginnings of the Big Bend Park." West Texas Historical Association *Year Book*, XLIV (October, 1968), pp. 3–14.

Pete Williams. "The Big Bend." *Sparks*, January, 1944, p. 5.

Conrad Wirth. "The Mission Called 66." *National Geographic*, CXXX (July, 1966), pp. 6–47.

Dee Woods. "The Dusty River Region." *South*, December, 1946, pp. 11, 23, 26.

Books

Robert J. Casey. *The Texas Border and Some Borderliners: A Chronicle and a Guide*. Indianapolis: The Bobbs-Merrill Company, Inc., 1950.

Frank Collinson. *Life in the Saddle*. Edited and arranged by Mary Whatley Clarke. Norman: University of Oklahoma Press, 1963.

F. Fraser Darling and Noel D. Eichhorn. *Man and Nature in the National Parks*. 2nd ed.; Washington, D. C.: The Conservation Foundation, 1969.

J. Frank Dobie. *The Longhorns*. New York: Bramhall House, 1941.

Robin W. Doughty. *Wildlife and Man in Texas: Environmental*

Change and Conservation. College Station: Texas A & M University Press, 1983.
William O. Douglas. *Farewell to Texas: A Vanishing Wilderness.* New York: McGraw-Hill Book Company, 1967.
William C. Everhart. *The National Park Service.* New York: Praeger Publishers, 1972.
Paul Horgan. *Great River: The Rio Grande in North American History.* New York: Rinehart and Company, Inc., 1954.
John Ise. *Our National Park Policy: A Critical History.* Baltimore: Johns Hopkins Press, 1961.
John R. Jameson. *Big Bend National Park: The Formative Years.* El Paso: Texas Western Press, 1980.
J. O. Langford with Fred Gipson. *Big Bend: A Homesteader's Story.* Austin: University of Texas Press, 1955.
Virginia Madison. *The Big Bend Country of Texas.* 2nd. ed.; New York: October House, Inc., 1968.
_____. and Hallie Stillwell. *How Come It's Called That? Place Names in the Big Bend Country.* rev. ed.; New York: October House, Inc., 1968.
Ross A. Maxwell. *The Big Bend of the Rio Grande: A Guide to the Rocks, Geologic History, and Settlers of the Area of Big Bend National Park.* Austin: University of Texas, Guidebook 7, Bureau of Economic Geology, 1968.
_____. John T. Lonsdale, Roy T. Hazzard, John A. Wilson. *Geology of Big Bend National Park, Brewster County, Texas.* Austin: University of Texas, publication no. 6711, Bureau of Economic Geology, 1967.
Maxine E. McCloskey, ed. *Wilderness the Edge of Knowledge.* New York: Sierra Club, 1970.
_____. and James P. Gilligan, eds. *Wilderness and the Quality of Life.* New York: Sierra Club, 1969.
Roderick Nash. *The American Environment: Readings in the History of Conservation.* Reading, Massachusetts: Addison-Wesley Publishing Company, 1968.
_____. *Wilderness and the American Mind.* rev. ed.; New Haven: Yale University Press, 1982.
National Parks for the Future. Washington, D. C.: The Conservation Foundation, 1972.
Carlysle Graham Raht. *The Romance of the Davis Mountains and*

Big Bend Country: A History. El Paso: The Rahtbook Company, 1919.

Alfred Runte. *National Parks: The American Experience*. Lincoln: University of Nebraska Press, 1979.

John Salmond. *The Civilian Conservation Corps, 1933-1942: A New Deal Case Study*. Durham: Duke University Press, 1967.

Robert Shankland. *Steve Mather of the National Parks*. 3rd. ed.; Alfred A. Knopf, 1970.

O. L. Shipman. *Taming of the Big Bend*. Marfa, Texas: privately published, 1926.

W. D. Smithers. *Chronicles of the Big Bend: A Photographic Memoir of Life on the Border*. Austin: Madrona Press, Inc., 1976.

Donald Swain. *Wilderness Defender: Horace M. Albright and Conservation*. Chicago: University of Chicago Press, 1970.

Texas: A Guide to the Lone Star State (Work Projects Administration Writers' Program). New York: Hastings House, 1940.

Ronnie C. Tyler. *The Big Bend: A History of the Last Texas Frontier*. Washington, D. C.: Department of the Interior/National Park Service, 1975.

William Vogt. *Road to Survival*. New York: William Sloane Associates, Inc., 1948.

Barton H. Warnock. *Wildflowers of the Big Bend Country, Texas*. Alpine: Sul Ross State University, 1970.

Roland H. Wauer. *Naturalists' Big Bend*. College Station: Texas A & M University Press, 1980.

Other Sources

An Alternative to the Master Plan and Wilderness Proposal for Big Bend National Park. Temple, Texas: Americans Backing Better Park Development, 1972.

Big Bend National Park: Final Environmental Statement; Proposed Wilderness Classification. Washington, D. C.: Department of the Interior/National Park Service, 1975.

Big Bend National Park Master Plan. Washington, D. C.: Department of the Interior/National Park Service, 1973.

Big Bend National Park Master Plan: Preliminary Draft. Washington, D. C.: Department of the Interior/National Park Service,

1971.

Big Bend: Official National Park Handbook. Washington, D. C.: Department of the Interior/National Park Service, 1983.

William E. Brown and Roland Wauer with the assistance of Roy E. Appleman and Benjamin Levy. *Historic Resources Management Plan: Big Bend National Park.* Washington, D. C.: Department of the Interior/National Park Service, 1968.

Clifford B. Casey. *Soldiers, Ranchers and Miners in the Big Bend.* Washington, D. C.: Department of the Interior/National Park Service, 1969.

Decisions of the United States Board of Geographical Names: Decisions Rendered Between July 1, 1938 and June 30, 1939. Washington, D. C.: Government Printing Office, 1939.

Guide to the Backcountry Roads and the River: Big Bend National Park. Big Bend Natural History Association, 1970.

Hearings before a Subcommittee of the Committee on Appropriations, House of Representatives, 93rd Cong., 1st sess., Part II; Department of the Interior and Related Agencies Appropriations for 1974. Washington, D. C.: Government Printing Office, 1973.

Hiker's Guide to the Developed Trails and Primitive Routes: Big Bend National Park. Big Bend Natural History Association, 1971.

Arthur D. Martinson. "Mountain in the Sky: A History of Mount Rainier National Park." Unpublished Ph.D. dissertation, Washington State University, 1966.

Part One of the National Park System Plan: History. Washington, D. C.: Department of the Interior/National Park Service, 1972.

Part Two of the National Park System Plan: Natural History. Washington, D. C.: Department of the Interior/National Park Service, 1972.

Road Guide to the Paved and Improved Dirt Roads: Big Bend National Park. Big Bend Natural History Association, 1969.

Douglas Hilman Strong. "A History of Sequoia National Park." Unpublished Ph. D. dissertation, Syracuse University, 1964.

Roger C. Thompson. "The Doctrine of Wilderness: A Study of the Policy and Politics of the Adirondack Preserve Park." Unpublished Ph. D. dissertation, Syracuse University, 1961.

U. S., Department of Interior. *Annual Reports of the Secretary of the*

Interior, for the fiscal years ended June 30, 1933, 1934, 1935.
   Washington, D. C.: Government Printing Office, 1933, 1934, 1935.
Wilderness Recommendation: Big Bend National Park, Texas.
   Washington, D. C.: Department of the Interior/National Park Service, 1973.
Wilderness Study: Big Bend National Park. Washington, D. C.: Department of the Interior/National Park Service, 1971.

Index

Adams, Dom, 26
Alaska, 113; the "last frontier", 51–52
Alberta, Canada, 113
Albright, Horace M.: concern of Director of National Park Service about establishment of inferior national parks, 4
Allred, Governor James V., 19–20, 26, 29, 61, 62; opposed to additional taxation, 22; vetoed appropriation measure, 22–23; reasons for appropriation veto, 24–25; honorary president of Big Bend Park Park Association, 28
Alpine *Avalanche*, 65
Alpine, Texas, 16, 26, 81, 101, 104
Alpine, Texas Chamber of Commerce, 124; Local Park Committees set up, 25, 26–27; proposal for international park, 113–114
Alps Mountains: compared with Big Bend's scenery, 50
Alto Frio Canyon National Park (proposed), 4
American Club, 122
American Museum of Natural History, 98
Amistad Reservoir, 111, 126
Apache]ndians, 56
Appalachian National Park, 39
Arizona, 87, 113
Argentina, 113
Asia, 50
Askew, Vestal, 90, 91

Austin, Texas, 28, 54

Banta Shut-In, 73
Bean, Judge Roy, 72
Big Bend (the boat), 58
Big Bend International Park (proposed), 50, 59–60, 72, 74–75; first proposed, 14, 15–16; used' as tool to lobby for appropriation, 24; A.W. Dorgan s proposal (sponsored by Alpine, Texas Chamber of Commerce), 113–114; E.E. Townsend's proposed sister park in Mexico, 114; Senator Morris Sheppard suggested idea to President Franklin Roosevelt, 114; Mexican plans for, 115; two conferences at El Paso, 115–116; joint commission appointed, 116; comparison of Mexican and U.S: sites, 116; meeting of international comm1ssion delayed by deaths of U.S. Park Service officials, 117; contrast of U.S. and Mexican national park policies, 119; Mexican antipathy towards U.S., 119–121; President Harry Truman's support for, 121–122; Texans' antipathy towards Mexico, 123–124; alleged hoof and mouth disease in, 124; Korean conflict and Cold War delayed negotiations for, 124
Big Bend Land Department, 42, 43, 44; organized by Texas State Parks Board to purchase land,

Index

Big Bend National Park, 1, 127; National Park Service unaware of, 6; E.E. Townsend first has idea for park, 9; recommended for national park by Roger Toll, 12-13; NPS Director Arno Cammerer approved Big Bend project, 13; Civilian Conservation.Corps camp in Chisos Basin, 10, 13, 27; international park, 14, 15-16, 133-126; Herbert Maier report, 14-15; enabling bills introduced in U.S. Congress, 16; enabling act passed, 16, 19; summary of reasons national park established, 17; mineral rights, 20; appropriation bill for, 21, 22-23; economic benefits, 22-23; economic arguments for, 32, 60-61, 66-67, 71, Governor James Allred vetoed appropriation for, 22-23; reasons for Governor Allred's appropriation veto, 24-25; Local Park Committees established, 26-27; Big Bend Park Association's fund raising efforts, 28-29, 32-34; threatened by vandals, 31, 36; beauty of landscape, 32; Texas Legislature passed appropriation for, 34-35; land purchase begun, 35-36; land acquisition, 39-48; development hampered, 36-37; Mission 66, 37, 79-80, 104-105; effect of World War II on, 41, 97; officially established, 46; publicitY campaign, 49-67; negative publicity, 52-53; publicitv movie, 54; "peace park", 50; planning and development of, 69-84; proposal for longhorn ranch, 72-74; concession contract awarded, 77, wilderness proposal, 80-84; predator controversy, 85-95; smuggling, 97, 105-106, 107; hoof and mouth disease, 97, 106, 107; wildlife threatened, 97-98; 40-41 archaeology and paleontology of, 98; selection of first superintendent, 99; life on the "last frontier", 99-112; morale problems of staff, 102; new place names, 103; raid on Glenn Springs, 105; violence at, 105; poaching at, 106; grass and forest fires at, 107; mysterious wildlife deaths at, 107-108; feral burros and goats at, 108; trespassing livestock, 108-109; threat of dam building at, 109-111, 117; treaty for U.S.-Mexican reservoir, 110-111

Big Bend National Park Development Committee, 81, 83

Big Bend Park Association, 31, 41, 44-45, 66; organized, 28; failure of, 33-34

Big Bend State Park, 97, 127; initially called Texas Canyons State Park, 10; Civilian Conservation Corps Camp at, 10

Bolton, Herbert E., 55

Boquillas Canyon, 40, 47, 110-111, 127; geographical landmark in Big Bend National Park, 6

Boquillas, Mexico, 76

Border Patrol, 56; relayed messages to park, 101

Boston, Massachusetts, 89

Brewster County, Texas, 30, 41, 43, 53, 65, 71, 91, 98

Brewster Countv, Texas Chamber of Commerce: set up Local Park Commi-ttees, 26-27

Brown, Rollo Walter, 62-63

Brownsville, Texas, 56

Bureau of Animal Husbandry, 106

Bureau of Reclamation, 110, 117

California, 54

California, University of, 55

Cammerer, Arno B., 17, 21, 24, 35, 60, 117; Director of National Park Service has reservations about Big

Index

Bend project, 13; approved Big Bend project, 13; authorized interdepartmental investigation of, 14
Canada, 50, 113
Carithers, Joe, 107
Carlsbad Caverns National Park, 6, 22
Carmen Mountains, 122
Carter, Amon, Sr., 31, 44–45; selected chairman of Big Bend Park Association, 28–29; began subscription campaign, 29; blamed for failure of Big Bend Park Association, 32–34; delayed delivery of deed, 36; favored land acquistion program, 41
Casner, Jim, 26
Castolon, 44, 46, 47, 81
Cauthorn, Albert R., 32
Ceniza Flat, 82
Century Magazine, 55
Chamizal controversy, 126
Chicago, 74
Chihuahua, Mexico, 107, 113, 118, 119, 122, 124
Chihuahua City, Mexico, 124
Chihuahuan Desert, 126
Chisos Basin, 13, 72, 76, 77, 78, 80, 82–83, 97, 104–105, 124, 129
Chisos Mountains, 27, 32, 36, 40, 49, 52, 63, 70, 73, 75, 76, 81, 88, 98, 107, 127, 129; geographical landmark in Big Bend National Park, 6
Cinco de Mayo (the boat), 58
Civil War, 86
Civilian Conservation Corps, 32, 36, 71, 76, 104, 107; creation of agency, 3; catalyst for establishment of state parks, 3; jobs for unemployed, 3; camp in Chisos Mountains, 10, 13, 27
Clark, Nolan, 63–64
Coahuila, Mexico, 107, 113, 119, 120, 122, 124
Cold War, 79

Colima Warbler, 49, 97–98
Colp, D.E., 8, 114
Comacho, Avila, 118, 121
Congressional Record, 16
Connally, Senator Tom, 124, 127; introduced Senate Bill 2131, 16
Coronado, 55
Coronado Memorial, 113, 123
Cumbres de Majalca National Park, 119

Dallas, Texas, 23, 54
Daniels, Josephus, 24, 115
Daniels Ranch, 76
Davis Mountains National Park (proposed), 4
Dead Horse Mountains, 4
Del Rio, Texas, 82
Demaray, Arthur, 30, 90, 91
Dinosaur National Monument, 109
Dobie, J. Frank, 74; wrote article in *Nature Magazine* that calls for park at Big Bend, 9; promoted Big Bend, 54–55; attacked Big Bend livestock interests, 89
Doran, Hilary, Jr., 82
Dorgan, A.W., 124; prepared plans for international park, 113–114
Drury, Newton B., 35, 42, 44, 45, 65, 74, 76, 93, 118, 120

Echevaria, Luis, 125
Eisenhower, Dwight, 79
El Paso, Texas, 56, 60, 89, 128
El Paso Times, 61
Emergency Conservation Work Agency. *See* Civilian Conservation Corps
Europe, 50
Everglades National Park, 6, 39

Falcon Reservoir, 111, 126
Ferguson, Governor "Ma", 10
Fish and Wildlife Service, 93–94, 121
Florida, 54
Foree, Kenneth, 65
Forest Service, 2

Index

Fort Stockton, Texas, 128
Fort Worth *Star-Telegram*, 23, 28, 36, 61; publicized Big Bend National Park, 25-26, 27
Fort Worth, Texas, 23
France, 43

Garcia, Roberto Garduno, 125
Garrison, Lon, 124
George, King of England, 59
Glenn Springs, 105
Gonzales, Miguel L., 120, 121
Graham Ranch, 76
Grand Canyon, 50
Grand Canyon National Park, 19n, 109
Grand Teton National Park, 61
Guadalupe Mountains National Park, 1, 4, 6

Haley, J. Evetts, 12
Hill, Milton, 62
Hill, Robert T., 55, 105; author of *Century Magazine* article on the Big Bend country, 9n
Hot Springs, 102-103
Howarth, George, 107
Hull, Cordell, 114-115
Humble Oil and Refining Company, 21, 33
Hunter, W.B., 41-42

Ickes, Harold, 13, 15, 36, 60, 114
Interior, Department of, 71
Interior, Secretary of, 77
International Boundary C85Cission, 111
Isle Royale National Park, 39

Jersey Lilly Saloon, 72

Kimsey, J. Edgar, 62
King, J. H., 41, 42
Kings Canyon National Park', 16, 109
Kiwanis, 66
Korean War, 36

KULF, Radio Station, 101

Lane, Joe, 57
Life Magazine, 52, 64-65
Literary Digest, 64
Lions Club, 66
Lufkin *Daily News*, 62

Maier, Herbert, 14-15, 20, 21, 24, 25, 30, 115
Mammoth Cave National Park, 29
Marathon, Texas, 101, 102
Marfa, Texas, 26, 62
Mariscal Canyon, 40, 62, 72, 110-111, 127; geographical landmark in Big Bend National Park, 6
Maxwell, Ross, 51, 65, 76, 77, 78, 90, 101, 102, 103, 107, 108-109, 111-112, 119; requested appropriation for land purchase, 47; reconciled predator controversy, 91-92, 93-94; first superintendent at Big Bend, 99
McKay, Douglas, 124-125
McKittrick Canyon National Park (proposed), 4
Mexican Department of Forestry, Fish, and Game, 115
Mexico, 97, 113
Mexico City, 118, 125
Midland, Texas, 82
Mission 66, 37, 79-80, 104-105
Morelock, Horace, 25, 50; publicized Big Bend National Park, 26; vice-chairman of Big Bend Park Association, 28
Mormons, 60
Morris, G.C., 35

Nail, Sam, 87
National Geographic, 54-55, 64, 79, 87-88
National Park Concessions, Inc., 77-78
National Park Service, 2, 19, 20, 21, 24, 27, 29, 30, 32, 34, 35, 36, 39, 42, 45, 46, 47, 48, 51, 52, 53, 56,

Index

60, 65, 69, 70, 73, 74, 83, 85, 87, 88, 89, 90, 91, 92, 95, 98, 99, 100, 101, 103, 111, 114, 115, 117, 118, 119, 121-122, 123, 125, 126, 127, 128, 129; six park sites proposed for Texas, 4; benefited from New Deal programs, 36; hired historian Walter Prescott Webb, 55-59; new master plan proposed for Big Bend, 80-81; wilderness proposal, 80-84; conflict with Fish and Wildlife Service, 93-94; Mission 66 improvements at Big Bend, 104-105; opposition to dams in national parks, 109-110; international parks proposed by, 113
Neff, Governor Pat, 2
New Deal, 60, 70-71
Newell, Johnny, 81, 83
Newsome, Carter "Buck", 82
Northwestern University, 99

O'Daniel, Mike, 30
O'Daniel, Molly, 30
O'Daniel, Pat, 30
O'Daniel, Governor W. Lee, 30, 31-32, 34, 59
Ohio, 44
Olympic National Park, 16
Organ Pipe Cactus Monument, 113

Palo Duro Canyon National Park (proposed), 1-2, 4
Pan American Highway, 124
Pan American Union, 119
Panther Junction, 75, 82, 101, 104; selected for park headquarters, 76
Parade Magazine, 64-65
Parque Nacional de la Gran Comba, 122, 125
Pearson, Drew, 53, 66-67
Pecos County, Texas, 86
Perez, Carlos Villes, 122-123
Persimmon Gap, 47, 129
Phillips, H.M., 90-91
Pierce, Richard H., 82

Pinchot, Gifford, 2, 115
Presidio County,- Texas, 53
Presnall, Clifford C., 121

Quevedo, Miguel A. de, 115

Rayburn, Sam, 24
Record, James R., 25
Red River Improvement Association, 1-2
Rio Grande, 14, 44, 46, 56, 58, 62, 70, 72, 75, 76, 77, 102, 105, 106, 110, 117, 121, 122, 124, 125-126
Rio Grande Village, 81, 82
River Riders, 106
Roark, Alf, 23
Rocky Mountain National Park, 22
Roosevelt, President Franklin D., 17, 19, 32, 36, 43, 59-60, 74, 118, 127; interested in international park at Big Bend, 15-16; "good neighbor" foreign policy, 113
Roosevelt, President Theodore, 115
Rotary International, 66

Saltillo, Mexico, 118, 124
San Angelo, Texas, 26, 41, 64
San Angelo *Standard-Times*, 88
San Antonio, Texas, 122
San Antonio *Express*, 61-62
San Francisco, California, 2
Santa Elena Canyon, 40, 50, 51, 56, 57, 59, 62, 81, 104, 110, 127; photograph, 5; geographical landmark in Big Bend National Park, 6
Saturday Evening Post, 64-65
Sheep and Goat Raisers Association, 89, 91, 92-93, 94
Sheep and Goat Raisers' Magazine, 87, 90-91
Shenandoah National Park, 25, 29
Sheppard, George H., 41
Sheppard, Senator Morris, 24, 52, 127; president, Red River Improvement Association, 2; promoted idea of national park, 3-

4; introduced international park idea to President Franklin Roosevelt, 15, 114; introduced Senate Bill 2131, 16
Shipman, Jimmie, 57
Sierra del Carmen Mountains, 118, 120, 121
Simpich, Frederick, 64
Skaggs, Thomas, 56, 57–58
Smith, Maggie, 102–103
Smith, Governor Preston, 81
Snelson, W.E., 82
Sonora, Texas, 108
Sonora (Mexican state), 113, 122
State parks, Texas, 2, 3
Stephens, Representative John H., 1–2
Sterling, Governor Ross, 2
Stevenson, Coke, 35–36, 44, 50; introduced unsuccessful state appropriation bill, 22, 23; extolled economic benefits of national park, 22–23; as Lieutenant Governor worked for successful appropriation, 30–31
Stinson, Jeff, 32
Story, Isabelle, F., 53
Sul Ross State Teachers College, 26, 50, 62
Swift, Roy, 62
Swift, W.E., 62

Tennessee Valley Authority, 110
Terlingua-Alpine Road, 101
Texas Canyons State Park, 10, 127
Texas Centennial, 23, 54
Texas Court of Civil Appeals, 41
Texas Federation of Women's Clubs, 1, 65–66
Texas Fish and Wildlife Department, 52
Texas Gulf Sulphur Company, 54
Texas Highway Department, 81, 82
Texas Legislature, 3, 8, 19, 21, 27, 34–35, 46, 47, 50, 59, 61
Texas Livestock Commission, 106
Texas National Park (proposed), 4, 8
Texas Parks and Wildlife Department, 81
Texas Permanent School Fund, 14–15, 16, 20–22, 24–25, 28, 31, 32, 35, 42, 128
Texas Rangers, 56
Texas State Board of Education, 21
Texas State Parks Board, 8, 14–15, 16, 23, 27, 31, 34, 35, 39, 40, 41–42, 44, 46, 64, 99, 114
Texas State Supreme Court, 41
Texas State Teachers Association, 21
Texas Tourist Development Agency, 81
Texas, University of, 55
Texon, Texas, 62
Thomason, Representative Ewing, 10, 13, 15, 27, 29–30, 127; introduced House Resolution 6373, 16
Thompson, Eugene "Shorty", 40–41, 42
Throckmorton, Texas, 41
Tillotson, Minor R., 34, 35, 44, 51, 71–72, 74, 76, 78, 119
Tisinger, Ben F., 21
Titanic, 58
Toll, Roger, 13, 17, 51, 127; recommended Big Bend for national park status, 12; biography of, 12–13; appointed to international park commission, 117; death, 117
Tolson, Hillory, 93, 122–123
Tornillo Flat, 73
Townsend, Everett Ewing, 17, 20, 21, 42, 44, 65, 127, 128; dreamed of park in Chisos Mountains, 9; introduced House Bill 771, 10; lobbied for national park, 10, 12; photograph, 11; discovered water in Chisos Basin, 13; lobbyist for National Park Service, 34; appointed project manager for land acquisition project, 39; completed land classification, 40;

Index

appointed assistant administrator of Big Bend Land Department, 40–41; conducted research for Walter Prescott Webb expedition, 56; favored dams in Big Bend, 110; suggested idea of companion park in Mexico, 114

Truman, President Harry S.: promoted international park, 121–122

U.S. Armv-, 105
U.S. Board of Geographical Names, 103
U.S. Border Patrol. *See* Border Patrol
U.S. Bureau of Reclamation. *See* Bureau of Reclamation
U.S. Coast Guard, 58
U.S. Department of Agriculture, 106
U.S. Fish and Wildlife Service. *See* Fish and Wildlife Service
U.S. Forest Service. *See* Forest Service
U.S. National Park Service. *See* National Park Service
U.S. State Department, 120, 122, 123
Utah, 60
Uvalde, Texas, 93

Vogt, William, 120

Wagstaff, R.M., 127; *Nature Magazine* article inspiration for park at Big Bend, 9; introduced House Bill 771, 10

Washington, D.C., 43
Waterton-Glacier Park, 50, 113
Webb, Mrs. Walter Prescott, 58
Webb, Walter Prescott: hired by National Park Service to publicize Big Bend, 55–59
Wegemann, Carroll, 51
West Texas Historical and Scientific Society, 89
Wichita Mountains Game Preserve, 73
Wilbur, Ray Lyman, 3–4
Wilderness Act (1964), 81–82
Williams, Ernest, 93
Williams, Pete, 64
Williams, Ray, 92
Winfield, H.L.: introduced appropriation bills, 22, 23, 31; supported additional appropriation, 46
Wirth, Conrad, 8, 15, 27, 77, 79, 125
Woodville, Texas *Booster*, 50
World War II, 36, 50, 53, 73, 79, 85, 118, 119
Wright, George M., 70; appointed to international park commission, 117; death, 117
Wychgel, Adrian, 29
Wychgel, Adrian, and Associates, 29
Wyoming, 61

Yellowstone National Park, 1, 50, 61, 128
Yosemite National Park, 109, 128

Zion National Park, 60

Gerald Myron Haslam

CLASH OF CULTURES
The Norwegian Experience with Mormonism, 1842-1920

American University Studies: Series IX (History). Vol. 7
ISBN 0-8204-0179-X   372 pages   hardcover US $ 39.80*

*Recommended price - alterations reserved

Herewith the definitive study of Norwegian Mormonism including the Story of «Sloopers» who converted in Fox River, Illinois; Mormon beginnings in Copenhagen; and - from there - the head-on clash of cultures in Norway between American religionists and Norwegian traditionalists - bishops, priests, justices, police authorities. The author draws heavily on documents in Norwegian archives (including Lutheran and Justice Department dossiers) and holograph Mormon journals to resurrect colorful characters such as district governor Christian Birch-Reichenwald; and describes Mormon-Thranite connections, the Supereme Court decision on «non-Christians» (1853), parliamentary debates through 1920, Church Department-Justice Department disagreement over the Mormon question, and Mormonism as instrument of social change. Here also the only comprehensive bibliography of Norwegian Mormonism and hundreds of translations from Norwegian documents (including complete Norwegian texts of all citations).

PETER LANG PUBLISHING, INC.
62 West 45th Street
USA - New York, NY 10036